CENTRAL
In Our Lives

WITHDRAWN

Donated to this library by
the Butler Center for Arkansas Studies,
a department of the Central Arkansas Library System,
and the Arkansas State Library

BUTLER CENTER
FOR ARKANSAS STUDIES

Also by Marvin Schwartz

History

In Service to America: A History of VISTA in Arkansas

Tyson: From Farm to Market

J. B. Hunt: The Long Haul to Success

Learning From The Land: How the YEA Program is
Developing a New Generation of Rural Leaders

People of the Land: A History of Arkansas
Land and Farm Development Corporation

Poetry

Passages

Poems for a Temporal Body

CENTRAL
In Our Lives

Voices from
Little Rock Central High School
1957-1959

**Ralph Brodie and
Marvin Schwartz**

The Butler Center for Arkansas Studies
Central Arkansas Library System • Little Rock, Arkansas

The Butler Center for Arkansas Studies
Central Arkansas Library System
100 Rock Street
Little Rock, Arkansas 72201

ISBN: 978-0-9708574-7-7 PB
ISBN: 978-0-9708574-8-4 HB

Front cover photo: Chere Lile Payne

Back cover: *Life* Magazine Cover, October 7, 1957,
    courtesy of John Bryson/Time & Life Pictures/Getty Images.

For additional information,
visit **www.centralinourlives.org**.

Printed in the United States of America.

Contents

Foreword by Ralph Brodie 11
Foreword by Marvin Schwartz 15

Acknowledgments. 17

Voices From Central High: Students and Teachers 19

Introduction 21
    History Has Many Faces 22
    The Role of Students. 23

Voices From Central High: In the Halls 25

Chapter 1. Making Choices, Choosing Sides 27
    Seeing the Harassment. 30
    Social Integration and Silence 33
    Do the Right Thing 35
    Academic Assistance. 40
    Tiger Articles and Editorials 42
    A Policy of "No Discussion" 46
        Involvement of Student Leadership 48
    The Troublemakers 49
        Problem Students. 51
        Limited Sanctions on Problem Students 54
    Media Truth and Distortions. 57
        Ira Lipman and John Chancellor 63

Voices From Central High:
    Mike Wallace Interview with Ralph Brodie 67

Chapter 2. Arkansas and the South **71**
   Understanding Southern Rhetoric 71
   Integration and Communism 74
   Southern Response: Massive Resistance
     and the Southern Manifesto 75
   Arkansas' Position 77
   School Board Decisions and Community Response 79
   Forces Arrayed against Central High 81
   All Deliberate Speed 84
   The Politics of Governor Orval Faubus 86
   Removal of the National Guard 88

Voices From Central High: On the School Grounds **91**

Chapter 3. The Consequences **95**
   The Students 95
   Threats to Families 101
   The Lost Year, 1958-59 105
   Harassment of Teachers 109
   The Purge of Teachers and the STOP Campaign 112
   Impact on the Community 116
   Apathy and Guilt 117
   Changes in the Heart 122

Voices From Central High: The Mob Outside **127**

Chapter 4. Personal Motivation **129**
   Student Values 129
   Academics and Citizenship 133
   Citizenship Training at Boys State and Girls State 136
   Parents and Community 138
   Athletic Victories and Legendary Success 144
   Wilson Matthews: Head Football Coach 146
   Lawrence Mobley: Head Basketball Coach 148
   Clyde Hart: Head Track Coach and Trainer 149

Voices From Central High:
  National Guardsmen and Airborne Troops 153

Chapter 5. The Burden of Ethics 157
  Doing Good for the Wrong Reasons. 159
  Piety and Self-Righteousness. 161
  The Search for Heroes. 163
  Preach a Little Love 165
  Closure 166

Appendices 169
  A. Selected Photographs 171
  B. Timeline of Desegregation at
        Little Rock Central High School 183
  C. Teacher and Student Contributors. 191
  D. Central High Teachers and
        Administrators Purged in May 1959 197
  E. Pentangle Service Board letter 199
  F. Index 201
  G. Chapter Notes. 205

About the Authors 211

Whenever I am asked to speak about my experience of being a student at LRCHS in 1957, the infamous year of desegregation, I become very anxious. I'm worried about questions such as: ...Will their preconceived notions about Southern racism prevent them from hearing that the majority of white students were, in fact, the unsung heroes who helped keep the classroom situation calm enough for the school year to proceed?

Jane Emery Prather, Class of 1958

Many of the white students who were disruptive were the same "problem" students from the year before; the difference was that now they had encouragement and approval from adults on the outside in their harassment of the black students. They handed out hate literature, and a few were relentless in their efforts to disrupt. I remember telling my homeroom students regularly, "Don't do anything today that you can't live with the rest of your life."

Shirley Swaim Stancil, Guidance Counselor

I changed to someone who felt a real sense of compassion for these students, and felt like they deserved something that I had. I think at that point is when I really began to change my mind and realize that this was not a states' rights issue, it was a people issue.

Craig Rains, Class of 1958

To my parents
Frank T. and *Hazel Gray Brodie*
and
twin sisters
Marilyn Archer and *Marilou Brodie*

RB

To *Sandy*,
my inspiration and my love

MS

ERRATA
For page 177
Caption on Bottom photo

After publication of the first edition of this book, the authors received information (from one of the young women in the photo) that the photo shown is not a posed photo. A photo similar to this, but taken by another photographer, was purported to be a posed photo. The authors wish to apologize for the mistaken identification of the photo on the bottom of this page.

The correct caption follows:

Unauthorized persons turned away:
A widely distributed image shows persons, assumed by the soldiers to have no business on school property, being moved away from the Central High School grounds. Photo courtesy of Arkansas Democrat-Gazette.

Foreword by Ralph Brodie

After 50 years, I feel compelled to explain what Little Rock Central High School means to me and, to some extent, to many other students who were there during that fateful 1957-58 school year. That is what this book is all about.

In writing this book, the very words of students who lived through the Central High Crisis are used. In some ways, no doubt, license has been taken in the manner and method by which the various quotations were grouped, labeled, and interpreted. The goal was to give the reader who had never thought much about the "third side" of this story a clearer window through which to see it.

Historians and the media have, perhaps naturally, focused on only two sides of this multi-faceted story: that of the Little Rock Nine and that of the problem students who opposed desegregation and bullied the Nine. The "third side" is the story about the other 1,850 students. It is a story that has been largely untold and, thus, almost completely overlooked. It is that story that we have tried to tell.

I do not, by this book, declare the story to be a highly dramatic one. Indeed, in most ways, it is not. Ironically, it is at its core a tale of good folks going on with their lives as they had before, accomplishing that which they were expected to accomplish when the year started, notwithstanding that the atmosphere around them was drastically different than it had ever been before. And it involves everyone's coming to a new understanding about law, justice, and our American way of life.

I have been accused at times of being too sensitive and defensive about a certain issue. That issue deals with the omission of the side of the other 1,850 students when the Central High story is told. This third side of the "Crisis" story reflects well on our student body.

As this book was about to go to print, a friend of mine who read the manuscript suggested that I seem to feel obligated not only to tell my story, but also to defend those 1,850 students against the negative historical light in which they continue to be cast. My plea? Guilty as charged.

It's true. I do think that the general view perpetuated over the years by most reporters and historians is that 100% of the white students at Central High in 1957-58 were in total opposition to the Little Rock Nine. Statements that it was "nine of them against 2,000 white students" and like phrases have been used so often in recent years that the rule, rather than the exception, has been to assume that there were just two opposing forces and nothing more.

The intent is not to tell 1,850 stories in this book, just one collective story with a hundred voices telling their part of it.

As a student body, those of us who were at Central High in the fall of 1957 were placed in what turned out to be a no-win situation. We were absolutely in the firing line as a troubled nation transitioned from the darkness of an era whose time had long since passed into what believers in the rule of law hoped would be a brighter time. The Supreme Court had ruled that a "more just society," one based on "equal opportunity" and "personal merit," meant integrated public schools. And, whether owing solely to the shenanigans of Governor Faubus or otherwise, Central High School occupied center stage in a drama in which most of us would just as soon not have been cast.

In my heart, I know that most of my fellow students and I met the major challenges of that year successfully, though not perfectly. In the most unusual and distracting year any faculty and student body could ever imagine, most of us did more than survive, we succeeded. And our successes, in objectively measurable areas, would make most schools envious even in a normal school year.

I know that many of my friends from the 1957-58 student body join me in saying that our only regret is that our newest students, the Nine, had to bear the harassment, bullying, and indignities that came their way that year. But we cannot change history.

I cannot let this book begin without citing the leadership and inspiration of those men and women who were our teachers, coaches, administrators, and friends at Central. In particular, Principal Jess W. Matthews, through calm and reasoned guidance, helped students keep their worlds and their lives together throughout Central's many trials. His wisdom, expressed often and clearly, succeeded far beyond what anyone could have hoped for. Thank you, Jess, for a life well lived with honor highly deserved. You and our remarkable teachers and coaches also deserve our highest praise for a job well done.

Our individual successes in our later lives are due in no small part to these individuals. In the final analysis, it is those teachers, those coaches, and that principal—all unrecognized heroes in my eyes—that this book ultimately honors. Thank you, dear friends, both living and departed. For it was you who made our alma mater "Central in our Lives."

> Hail to the old gold
> Hail to the black
> Hail alma mater
> Naught does she lack
> We love no other, so let our motto be
> Victory! Little Rock Central High

Alma Mater, Little Rock Central High School

Ralph Brodie
Student Body President, 1957-58
Little Rock Central High School Class of 1958

Foreword by Marvin Schwartz

Nearly 40 years ago, as I was about to leave my home in New York, my father gave me some advice for living in the South.

Because he thought Jews were not common in that region, he said people were likely to view me with some suspicion and ask, "Where are your horns?" The question reflected his experience with an urban legend originating with Michelangelo's Renaissance statue of Moses and the misinterpreted Biblical description of shafts of light emanating from his forehead. My father also cautioned me that Southerners would label me a "damn Yankee," a non-negotiable title that defined my distant heritage and permanent outsider status among them.

Years would pass before I realized how the simplicity of those terms undercut the complexity of real experience. In the urgency of our need to understand and attach meaning, we reduce people and issues to simple categories. Those patterns have value, but as Deborah Baldwin, Dean of the College of Arts, Humanities, and Social Sciences at the University of Arkansas at Little Rock, jokingly warns researchers, it is impossible to have a short conversation with a historian.

Today, through the recollections of men and women in their mid-to-late sixties, we are given an opportunity to reflect on a year in their teenaged lives when the world they knew and the expectations they held were lost in the sweeping actions of a few tumultuous months.

The bulk of Central High School students and faculty in 1957 did not draw the attention of the television camera, the newest and most powerful high-tech tool of the time. Yet their stories add to our full understanding of how ordinary people reacted and how they were judged. Their stories also reveal how a strident and militant minority can seize the day and overwhelm an inclusive process of understanding.

Interestingly, the more than one hundred student stories gathered for this work tell remarkably similar tales of a year filled with uncertainty and danger. Many of the stories are told here for the first time. These include the recollections of my co-author, Ralph Brodie. Because his story is such an integral part of the larger history, I have written his statements in a third-person style. In his direct

15

quotes, Ralph speaks through this book in the same manner as his former classmates.

Fifty years ago, these students were reluctant to share their views because of the potential for harsh retaliation. More recently, their reticence came from seeing their statements distorted or used to support preconceived positions. Usually, only parts of the story were told, and those were mostly the negative parts. This book endeavors to fill in those missing parts and to tell about that year at Central High as the students lived and experienced it. That year was full of unreported positive conduct and accomplishment in the midst of major social upheaval.

In this venerable anniversary year, the voices of a living history offer unique and individual perspectives that may challenge culturally comfortable and established interpretations. With the whole truth as its objective, this inclusive retrospective can help us learn from the past, overcome old errors and guilt, and move forward with a more holistic understanding of our collective history. The time for listening and learning has not ended.

Marvin Schwartz
Little Rock, Arkansas

Acknowledgments

This book was made possible by people who, as teenagers fifty years ago, met life's challenge and who, as adults, shared their personal stories about Central High.

Encouragement, support, and assistance have come from many quarters and many friends. Most significantly, members of the extended Brodie family—parents no longer with us and sisters who continue to share their love—have provided a lifetime of positive influence.

My thanks go to many classmates whose love for Central has been exhibited time and again with their continuing efforts to see that this book was written and told accurately. Chief among them are Craig Rains, Janice Shepherd Swint, Jane Emery Prather, Helen Ruth Smith Towns, Justlyn Matlock, and Georgia Dortch Sowers.

Many talented friends assisted in this book project and provided encouragement over the years. Special thanks goes to Ann Priddy, a teacher's teacher who was always the first to volunteer to review the manuscript; noted historian Elizabeth "Betsy" Jacoway; and documentary filmmaker Sandy Hubbard. Elizabeth Searcy reviewed and edited all the original stories submitted, and Central High School teacher George West was extremely helpful in bringing this work to completion.

This book would not have been written except for John Gill who recognized the importance of preserving these previously untold stories and provided key leadership in supporting the book's creation.

Encouragement to tell the whole story also came from Nancy Rousseau and Virgil Miller, who co-chaired Little Rock's Commission to commemorate the 50th Anniversary of the desegregation of Little Rock Central High School. For over four years, under their watchful guidance, the Commission planned the many events surrounding the September 25, 2007 event.

The authors are grateful to David Stricklin at the Butler Center for Arkansas Studies for his organization's role as publisher of this work and for the ongoing service to Arkansas as repository of Central High School stories.

Readers of the manuscript have provided invaluable editorial insight as these stories were transformed from a loose assembly of individual recollections into a cohesive portrait. Gratitude is expressed to the following people for that assistance: Annie Abrams, Marilyn Brodie Archer, Marilou Brodie, Bill and Kaye Burton, Charles "Chuck" Chappell, Vic Fleming, Jim and Charlotte Gadberry, Annette Hawkins, Pastor Randy Hyde, Glennys Oakes Johns, Walter M. Kimbrough, Margaret Kolb, Ira Lipman, Justlyn Matlock, Jerry McConnell, Bruce Moore, Virgil Miller, Walter Nunn, Frances Mitchell, Harriett Phillips, Jane Emery Prather, Ann Priddy, Mary K Priddy, Craig Rains, Paul Redditt, Ron Robinson, Nancy Rousseau, Wendell Ross, M.D., Sandy Schwartz, Katherine Searcy, Georgia Sowers, Tracey Steele, Mayor Mark Stodola, Janice Shepherd Swint, Martin Swint, Ted & Lou Ellen Treadway, Helen Ruth Smith Towns, Jim & Pat Wallace. The authors give all credit for the clarity of our story to these fine readers, but take total responsibility for any errors or omissions that remain in the book.

Voices From Central High: Students and Teachers

On September 23, the crowd grew in front of the school with screaming so-called adults. Early in the day I had a class in one of the third floor rooms that was closest to the street in front of the school. The windows were open since we did not have air-conditioning. The mob was so noisy you literally could not hear each other talk unless you shouted into someone's ear. Needless to say, we did not accomplish anything in that class that day.

Lloyd Erickson, Class of 1958

It was frightening going to school as a sophomore with yelling and screaming adults being held back by police, numerous reporters trying to get a story, and checking the radio and newspapers to see if the school would be open each day along with bomb scares and evacuations.

Student Name Withheld

The crowds outside Central High grew larger, and the local police were unable to prevent some from entering the building. They opened classroom doors, yelling they were looking for n****s. These were not necessarily Little Rock citizens, and it soon became clear, not only were they from out of town, but many came from out of state. Some of the mob attacked members of the press who happen to be black. I witnessed some of this from my window in the guidance office.[1]

Shirley Swaim Stancil, Guidance Counselor

19

When we changed classes, students saw teachers, counselors, principals, and soldiers walking the halls among us, ever watchful. If the teachers were not walking the halls, they were at their classroom doors watching. In my mind's eye, I can still see our principal, Mr. Matthews, with his distinguished carriage and striking white hair, walking those halls. As an adult I now can look back and only imagine the burden they felt to keep things on an even keel for the hundreds of students who were their responsibility.

Avay Gray Jaynes, Class of 1960

Not everything in '57-58 was gloom and doom, though. I have fond memories of the Friday night dances, the senior prom, and the nationally known entertainers who came to the school for programs. Vaughan Monroe brought his group twice for a program in the auditorium. I remember Bill Haley and the Comets coming to perform for us. He had some top hit records at the time, and we really rocked the auditorium.

Margaret Johnson Swaty, Class of 1958

Introduction

> Whenever I am asked to speak about my experience of
> being a student at LRCHS in 1957, the infamous year
> of desegregation, I become very anxious. I'm worried
> about questions such as: Will people label me a red-
> necked segregationist because I was even living in
> Arkansas at this time? Will the audience know anything
> about the history of segregation throughout the United
> States in the 1950s? Will their preconceived notions
> about Southern racism prevent them from hearing that
> the majority of white students were, in fact, the unsung
> heroes who helped keep the classroom situation calm
> enough for the school year to proceed?
>
> Jane Emery Prather, Class of 1958

This book is not a recently-started project fifty years after the fact.
Much of the commentary presented here has been prepared over several decades by Central High alumni who documented their personal histories for their families and, in the cases of those who became
educators, for their students.

By providing new information and analysis on a complex social
and historical event, this book will challenge certain interpretations
and categorizations. Through the voices of Central High's students
and teachers, in the factual review of the events and achievements of
that year, this book seeks to dispel half-truths and shallow stereotypes.
It seeks to enhance a national consciousness through a more complete
and more accurate understanding of this complex and inspiring story.

Within a significant episode in American history, this book aims
for a new insight into our common heritage. It will remind us that
history is a complex blend of social and political forces, rarely fitting
into easily defined segments. It will further remind us that in times of
dramatic social change, history can be unfair to those who quietly live

their lives, who are not vocal, who uphold traditional ethics and values, and whose values are different from the values of the time in which they are living.

> All the allegations of violence, threats of physical harm, and the descent of the media upon the school were an attempt to stage or create a crisis that did not exist .... This legacy of contrived negativity [has created] a fictitious reality and history that was eagerly accepted by the public.
>
> Joe Matthews, Class of 1958

History Has Many Faces

> In 1984 a foreign exchange student from New Zealand, upon learning that she would be spending a year of her life in some strange place called Little Rock, Arkansas, went to her local library and searched through its encyclopedias. In all of her library, the only reference she could find was a single negative paragraph about desegregation of Central High School in 1957 and the people in Little Rock and Arkansas.
>
> Avay Gray Jaynes, Class of 1960

History books and other publications have fostered the impression that no white teacher or student deserves positive portrayal for their actions during the tumultuous school year, 1957-1958, when Central High was desegregated. A compelling photograph contributes much toward that conclusion. One of the most famous photos in American history, and perhaps one of the most shameful, was taken in the streets outside Central High by *Arkansas Democrat* photographer Will Counts.

It shows an angry white teenager, Hazel Bryan Massery, her face an emblem of rage, taunting a black girl shortly after the girl was denied entry to Little Rock Central High School by a member of the Arkansas National Guard. The student, Elizabeth Eckford, walks away in profound dejection, her school books held close to her chest, her eyes fixed on the ground before her on that bright September morning as the surrounding crowd of white people watch her with glaring mistrust.

The photo captures in unquestionable detail the mean-spiritedness of those who resisted the first incidents of what was to become a national movement for civil rights. As a result, the single white girl's actions have come to represent the behavior and attitude of nearly 2,000 students and teachers inside Central High through the rest of the year.

One truth of the 1957 photo is the captured rage of the white teenager. But a parallel truth remains untold. Massery's rage did not epitomize the attitudes and actions of the administrators, teachers, coaches, and most students inside Central High. In fact, after October 1, 1957, Massery was no longer a Central High student, having withdrawn and re-enrolled at an all-white school outside Little Rock.

But the truth has many faces, seen and unseen. And like quiet acts of kindness and compassion unknown to anyone beyond those immediately involved, the truth can be lost in the clamor of the crowd and in our urgency to understand what we see.

The Role of Students

> People are under the opinion that inside the school was total chaos. It was not.
>
> Charles Evans Forte, Class of 1958

The role of students in what did and did not happen inside Central High can be understood through the memories of persons immediately involved, including comments from the black students known as the Little Rock Nine. The stories share the common observation that most of Central High's students were committed to academics and citizenship. Much of this commentary has not been included in other published works, leaving the traditional history of the events of 1957 in a sort of exclusiveness that does not do justice to the past. Many former students have been reluctant to tell their stories because of issues of personal privacy. Among the stories that have been told, many have been rejected by the media as biased and self-serving.

Minnijean Brown Trickey, one of the Little Rock Nine who has become an outspoken advocate for civil rights, expressed a concern about inclusiveness in communicating what she and her black classmates stood for nearly fifty years ago. "This is not Black history," she said. "This is American history."[2]

The intent of this book is to add to the historical record a set of voices that have largely been left out of it. Students at Central High were keenly aware their school was at the epicenter of an explosive situation. Yet 95 percent of them chose a daily pattern of positive behavior. Through deliberate measures, they were able to focus on and achieve for Central High and themselves not just a year of normalcy, but a year of exceptional school accomplishment. Very few histories of the crisis credit them with this action. We do this in the same spirit expressed by Trickey, the spirit of a full accounting of American history.

> For all that the history books have reflected and distorted, ... for all the criticism that we have endured, we know in our hearts that we handled it well. We know, because we were there.
>
> Carolyn Glover Hirby, Class of 1960

Voices From Central High: In the Halls

The day [Monday, September 23] was absolute chaos when the nine black kids first came to school without the National Guard to prevent them from entering or to protect us from the mob. As soon as the mob outside learned that they were inside the school, there was pandemonium in the halls. People, non-students, running up and down the halls of Central looking for them, yelling "They're in, they're in" and "We're going to kill those n****." It was frightening and I was scared to death. I had never seen anything like it before.

At that time, I excused myself from the class I was in, went to Principal Matthews' office, and called my dad [the Mayor] at City Hall. The message to my father was very simple. I told him, "Dad, if you don't get these kids out of here, someone's going to get killed."

He told me not to leave the principal's office, that he was sending a police car for me. He did, and I spent the rest of that day at City Hall. Obviously, the small police force of Little Rock was undermanned, not trained in riot control, and things were out of hand.

The next day, I was in my dad's office at City Hall when he sent the telegram to President Dwight Eisenhower asking for help.

Woody Mann, Class of 1958

I remember one morning Mr. J. O. Powell, Vice Principal for Boys, and I were checking restrooms in the basement, and when we came out there were two men in the hall. When we confronted them, they became belligerent and were told to leave the building. We felt sure that they were looking for the black students.

We had many fire drills due to bomb scares, some days up to three. On many occasions, I was called at home late at night to come to school and open lockers for firemen to search them. One night a locker down near the lunchroom in the basement did contain some type of explosive, which the firemen confiscated. Those were trying days.

Paul Magro, Industrial Arts Teacher

Inside the school, the black students were moved from class to class down the halls in a diamond formation of four of the 101st soldiers and the student in the middle of the formation.[3] You had to get against the walls to let the formation pass. The attitude of the soldiers was, in my opinion, too stern, but I am sure this was the way they were ordered to act and probably the only way it could be done.

Charles Evans Forte, Class of 1958

As the days passed, I never saw or experienced any commotion inside the building, yet upon returning home each day, I was greeted by concerned neighbors who had been watching the news on television. My homeroom was on the ground floor near 14th street; no students climbed out our windows, and our halls were free from disturbances. We were not allowed to go near the windows to watch the mayhem occurring on the corners of Park and 14th.

Helen Ruth Smith Towns, Class of 1958

Chapter 1

Making Choices, Choosing Sides

I think we as a student body tried to diligently maintain our composure, tried to conduct our lives with dignity and not become involved in the obvious-for-attention episodes.

Jackie Davis March, Class of 1960

Before school started that year, Preacher Dick Hardie at Westover Hills Presbyterian Church assembled a group of us who lived in west Little Rock. He encouraged us to be friends to the black students. He told us how important it was going to be for us to be supportive. He said it was going to be frightening.

Barbara Barnes Broce, Class of 1958

Students at Central High had been educated to make their own choices. Their teachers had discussed works of literature and history, encouraging an analytical understanding and an objective perspective. Their government and community leaders had identified a prudent, multi-year desegregation path to be followed, a plan of lawful compliance. And within their own ranks, student leaders had been reminded of their capacity for peer influence and encouraged to act in an appropriate manner.

Students understood their way of life was changing. The formal rhetoric of the Southern Manifesto and the inflammatory sermons of a few preachers had issued a battle cry against that change. But most Central High students did not believe that the enrollment of blacks in their school warranted the uproar. They accepted the fact that integration was going to happen. Most did not see it changing their lives, their attitudes, or their world at Central High.

> I did not anticipate the significance which would be placed on the integration of Central High. The issue of integration just was not that important to us. Of course, there were a few very vocal idiots who were adamantly opposed to integration, but I never talked to them about anything anyway.
>
> Charles Oakley, Class of 1958

"The momentous years during which we all became reluctant witnesses to history," as Charles "Chuck" Chappell called it, engaged students in decision-making they would have preferred to avoid. Teenagers generally are more inclined toward analysis of personal affairs than they are about analysis of political affairs. Their minds are quick; their reflexes agile. They are less interested in interpretation and more interested in response, more reactive than proactive. Central High students showed little concern about the long term social impact of school integration. Aware that change was upon them, they were faced with learning to deal with it on a daily basis.

> A Little Rock father called to report his son's reaction to the opening day at Central High. "Are you afraid to go to school," the father asked the boy as he prepared to pass through a cordon of armed National Guardsmen. "Yes," the boy replied. "What are you afraid of?" "Latin," was the boy's reply.
>
> Arkansas Gazette, September 5, 1957

Justlyn Matlock, describing the options available to students when facing powerful social forces, said that Central High students could neither overcome nor escape the forces of chaos or anger. Nor were they part of the forces mobilized in response. Their best option, she believed, was simply to stay out of the way.

We've all been taught to stay out of the way when a medical team is on the scene at a traffic accident. Trying to intervene in that situation can create more problems. This is the choice most of us made in 1957 at Central High. Professional forces were mobilized because of the threat of anger and chaos. Many of us had no animosity and wanted to help make the situation better for everyone, but we didn't know how. Ultimately, we decided that any attempt to intervene had the potential for causing more harm. So, we went about our role as students and left the confrontation with anger and chaos to the professional forces.

Justlyn Matlock, Class of 1958

The Class of 1958's first choice came in the spring of 1957. As junior students who lived in the enrollment district of the new Hall High, they could transfer for their senior years to the school that would open that fall. Hall would not be desegregated until 1959. By transferring, they would attend an all-white high school and effectively avoid personal involvement in any potential problem over desegregation or integration, as some were beginning to call it.

In the Spring of 1957, Central High's junior class had approximately 730 students. Approximately half, some 365, were eligible for the transfer. Of that group, 130 students made the switch to Hall High and 235 chose to remain at Central High. The Central High graduating class of 1958 included 603 students. Therefore, more than one third of them (235 of 603) had made the deliberate choice a year earlier to participate in the desegregation process.

The second choice presented to the future seniors, the Class of 1958, was how important they thought the issue of school desegregation was to their lives. The relatively low value attached to this event may be attributed to a characteristic teen-aged detachment, a nonplussed "nothing-bothers-me" attitude, a pose of coolness. But the students have repeatedly said they did not see the situation with the same level of importance adults assigned to it. In comparison to having a successful senior year, school desegregation was of little importance. Many of them had more immediate things on their minds.

> With time, we all went right on with football games, pep assemblies, class plays, going steady, breaking up, making up, and hours on the phone. We watched American Bandstand and loved rock-n-roll like every other high school kid in America. We were just kids, and kids are champions when it comes to adjusting .... bayonets and all!
>
> Carolyn Glover Hirby, Class of 1960

The third and ultimate choice made by Central High students was how they individually acted as the changes took place around them. Ultimately, every student was responsible for his or her own actions.

At the 40th anniversary reunion of the Central High Class of 1958, Little Rock Mayor Jim Dailey proclaimed a day of honor and remembrance for the former students who exhibited dignity in crisis and made sacrifices to uphold the values of society and education. A large majority of the senior class, he stated, displayed outstanding citizenship in honoring the law of the land.[4]

The formal language of the proclamation elevates day-to-day actions to a lofty pedestal. Such is the purpose of political rhetoric. Back in the hallways of Central High, crowds of students swarmed the corridors and stairways, their banter and laughter reflecting the commonality of their lives. No one, those voices might have told us, was consciously trying to be a hero or thought heroism might be required.

Seeing the Harassment

Many students insist they saw no incidents of harassment of black students, that they had only secondhand knowledge or rumors that such incidents took place. These statements have been interpreted by some as, at best, a cover for noninvolvement, and, at worst, a denial that harassment actually took place. Neither interpretation is valid.

Central High is an extremely large building, two blocks long and five stories tall, affording many covert or crowd-concealed opportunities for racist gestures. Acts of meanness and bullying were done by individuals or small groups of students, and often done in secret or falsely claimed as accidental. Second, white students, as well as faculty, who were not eyewitnesses to the incidents had no chance to directly intervene.

Principal Jess Matthews affirmed this situation in a speech to a Beta Club meeting in April 1958 when he said most teachers and students "have gone about their regular school program without knowledge of any incidents until they read about them in the newspapers."[5]

For the most part, however, student leaders—the school officers, club members, and athletes—felt a sense of readiness, a level of preparation adequate for the situation. A Central High coach recalled several summer meetings with the Key Club, a leadership group of the school's top boys, to prepare club members for their potential assistance in the desegregation process. But school officials, fearing reprisals against involved students, ultimately decided not to use organized and sponsored activities by any student group.

Elizabeth Eckford, in a 2004 interview with CNN, reflected on the complexity of the time and its capacity to leave differing memories, when she said, "People around me didn't react to what they saw or what they had to have heard. They turned their backs. It was impossible to have a friend." In the same interview, however, Eckford also recalled two white students who persistently befriended her in a speech class and made her feel that she belonged. "At the end of the day," she said, "two people treated me like a human being (starts to cry). And when they just... they persisted in talking to me every day like any other student. They didn't ask me something to see what it sounded like. They just talked to me."

Elizabeth Eckford and I had speech class together. The first day, she was sitting by herself away from everyone else. I realized how lonely she must have felt and what courage it took to be there. I went over and

31

sat by her. We were often speech partners and became life-long friends.

Ann Williams Wedaman, Class of 1959

The speech class of Mrs. Shirley "Micky" McGalin Dunaway allowed students to express some personality and individualism. Some of those moments were transforming for all involved.

I recall speaking to Elizabeth Eckford in the hall and on several occasions chatting with her before our speech class began. One day when Elizabeth was giving a speech, I was consciously listening to her with all the sincere attention I could muster. Suddenly, she burst out laughing, and said, "Wendell, would you please close your mouth!" We all laughed, I blushed as I often do, and it was refreshing and good for the whole class, including Elizabeth. I did not know that my mouth was wide open, but at least that moment we were all a class and shared a common joy.

Wendell Ross, Class of 1959

The memories of single incidents of friendship between black and white students are just one component of the larger memory of school activities and personalities. Ross' "moment of common joy" and Eckford's memory of two friendships neither deny nor eliminate the cumulative memories of unpleasant recurring experiences that black students and some of the white students share. The students' experiences, their highs and lows, are part of the complexity of memory which can call up a single image or a series of events with equal facility. No single incident in their personal histories and, similarly, no single perspective on history can tell the whole story.

Social Integration and Silence

> I truly don't recall much in the way of interaction with any of the black students. They were escorted between classes by troops and never seemed to talk to anybody. In that sense, I don't think we ever did actually "integrate."
>
> Charles E. "Chuck" Bell, Class of 1960

Little Rock's school desegregation strategies did not address the psychological issues that inevitably accompanied the new student relationships, and social integration was not a factor in the Little Rock School Board plan. Just getting black students into the classrooms of one all-white school was challenging enough. But in the mind of its staunch opponents, school desegregation was a first step toward race-mixing, an issue of the highest concern to segregationists. The Supreme Court decisions offered no guidance in this area. Schools were simply required to place black and white students in the same classrooms. What happened after that was up to them.

Within the school system, no preparation was made to help offset the initial, cautious distance between black and white students. Black students had been screened and selected with some attention to their psychological readiness for the challenge. But outside the counseling and support provided each afternoon to the Little Rock Nine by Daisy Bates, little is known about how each black student developed a personal response.

Several white students commented that members of the Little Rock Nine were quiet, shy, or kept to themselves. Chuck Bell recalled a classroom incident where he attempted to sit at a vacant desk beside one of the black girls. After being repeatedly told by the girl, "You don't have to sit there," Bell changed his seat to another part of the room. This incident illustrates that some of the black students, like many of the whites, found it easier to keep a safe distance from people they didn't know, understand, or trust.

School psychologists and counselors today recognize the enormous benefits of support groups, role-playing sessions, and discussions addressing the difficult private decisions that arise when people interact in new settings or experience trauma. Deprived of those types of psychological processing and preparation, some Central High students still hold deep emotions of pain and anger, fear and guilt. Kay Kuehnert Kennedy recalled a recent dinner with former classmate Linda Vassaur Schmidt when the women finally realized the long-term impact of that silence.

> Suddenly, we looked at each other and said, "We've never talked about this to each other." And it was true. Although, we've been friends since age twelve, we had never discussed it. That's the way it's always been—even back in school. We all kept our mouths shut because there was no reason to discuss it. We were at the mercy of history.
>
> Kay Varina Kuehnert Kennedy, Class of 1958

Encouraging discussion was an approach used at some churches, but it was not part of the school experience at Central High. The lack of guided dialogue between adults and students is reflected in a lengthy discussion between a former Central High student and an elderly Daisy Bates in 1995. At the time, Helen Ruth Smith Towns was a middle school teacher, and she was accompanying one of her former students to a meeting with Bates. The black student's history project on Central High later won second place in a national competition.

> "And what did you do to help any of the black students?" Daisy Bates said to me. I told her I was never a part of any harassment of the black students, that I had shared my algebra book with Gloria Ray when she did not have one, and that I had, upon entering algebra class before the other students arrived, and upon seeing a most unkind, racist depiction of Gloria drawn on her desk in chalk, quickly found an eraser and cleaned off the desk. I then

asked Ms. Bates, "What did you do or what did any other adult do to prepare the white students for what we were going to face during the coming year?" Her voice fell silent, and from that point on, I saw a positive change in her demeanor toward me. She had no answer.

Helen Ruth Smith Towns, Class of 1958

Do the Right Thing

Most people decided that, while they weren't prepared to be a flag-waving advocate for change, they would go about their business and do the right thing.

Charles E. "Chuck" Bell, Class of 1960

With 95 percent of the people inside Central High ready to obey the law, numerous examples of that involvement can be expected. A conscientious faculty and an achievement-oriented student body should have left some record of their commitment. That record does exist, and it contains numerous incidents of successful or thwarted efforts, illustrating what Pulitzer Prize-winning historian Taylor Branch called the "scrupulous rectitude" of most teachers and most of the white students.[6]

Can You Meet The Challenge?

Today the world is watching you, the students of Central High. They want to know what your reactions, behavior, and impulses will be concerning a matter now before us. After all, as we see it, it settles down to a matter of interpretation of law and order. Will you be stubborn, obstinate, or refuse to listen to both sides of the question? Will your knowledge of science help you determine your action or will you let customs, superstition, or tradition <u>determine the decision for</u> <u>you?</u> ...The challenge is yours, as future adults of America, to prove your maturity and intelligence and ability to make decisions by how you react, behave, and conduct yourself in this controversial question. What is your answer to this challenge?

Editorial by Jane Emery Prather,

<u>The Tiger</u> Co-Editor, September 19, 1957

The students and teachers did what good citizens do in times of crisis. They assumed their responsibility was not only to obey the law and encourage others to do likewise, but also to do all they could to make the best of confusing and complicated times and events beyond their control.

Emery's "challenge" took on greater meaning once the soldiers of the 101st Airborne were in place at the school. On September 25, the first morning after the troops' arrival, Major General Edwin Walker spoke at a student assembly. Nearly 850 students were absent from school that day, some as a protest to the desegregation or some as a result of parental concerns for their safety.[7] So, about 40 percent of the student body was missing when Walker explained his zero-tolerance policy for student dissenters, stating "I am here to execute the President's orders. My men are well trained and determined to carry out orders."[8] He told the students that no one would interfere with their coming or going or the peaceful pursuit of their studies. "This integration plan became a law that must be executed," Walker continued. "You are well-intentioned, law-abiding citizens. You need not be afraid of the soldiers, as they will not interfere with the school or its plans."

Moments after the assembly began, the Little Rock Nine entered the school guarded by twenty paratroopers. Outside, the mob continued screaming. A segregationist who refused a soldier's orders to disperse got his head bloodied by a rifle butt and his photo on the front page of that afternoon's *Arkansas Democrat*.

Back inside the school, student response to General Walker's comments was succinctly expressed by Brodie who, as student body president, had introduced him. Brodie responded, telling the General and the assembled students, "Central High students are proud of their athletic and scholastic records. We will be, and are, good citizens."[9]

> A number of years later, I was in Vietnam when we received a replacement officer from the states. We discovered that he had been at Little Rock with the 101st, as the general's bodyguard. He related to me that he had a real appreciation for the 2,000 or so students who didn't riot, rebel, or otherwise resist the court ruling.
>
> Charles E. "Chuck" Bell, Class of 1960

Directives from school administrators were very clear. Students and teachers were instructed to maintain order, avoid publicity, and, at all costs, avoid or immediately contain any confrontation. The intention behind these guidelines was equally clear. Central High officials knew that any disruption inside the school would fuel the crisis. A breach of order could essentially shut down the school.

The intensity of the segregationist position was demonstrated daily by the crowds outside the school and the political and community influence of the Capital Citizens Council and the Mothers' League of Central High. School officials believed that any overt acts supporting desegregation that were more than absolutely necessary would be leveraged by the opposition to provoke an even greater outcry. School administrators also believed that any school-sanctioned desegregation activity might expose the involved students and teachers to dangerous retribution.

Some analysts of social reform believe that basic ethical and moral behavior cannot overcome overt acts of aggression, that a more direct response is necessary. Seeking examples of that direct response in Central High students, they are critical of the white students for their lack of obvious interventions in the harassment of the black students. Yet the white students were repeatedly told they could have a successful year by just doing the right thing, by acting normal, which in the context of the time simply meant being respectful and not causing disruptions. Most of them did that, but some went beyond the norm. Through quiet and unheralded acts of kindness, some students were able to counterbalance the weight of intolerance and fear.

I think we did not know what to do, except to say [to the black students] you are welcome at our table at lunch, you can share my locker if it will help you, I will help with your class if possible.

One of the Little Rock Nine had her locker vulgarly desecrated by some boys. I mentioned to her that she was welcome to use my locker. I gave her my locker combination. I tried to be unobtrusive, hoping that she would be able to have some place for her things, and we would tell no one about it.

In the senior high fellowship at Westover Hills Presbyterian Church [of Preacher Dick Hardie], we had discussed frequently how segregation on the basis of race was offensive and wrong. So when some of the black students had the same lunch period with several of our fellowship members, Ralph Cotham and I let them know that they were welcome to sit at our lunch table. They accepted with a smile.

Glennys Oakes Johns, Class of 1958

To say that it was a quiet year and nothing much happened would be far from the truth. The black students were harassed and baited, pushed and tripped far more times than wound up in official incident reports. But there were positive interactions when they mixed with groups of tolerant white students and shared calm and reflective moments.

Before classes began in the morning, some students would gather in one of the study halls for Chapel Club.

It was a brief time for scripture reading, a devotional speaker, and a song. Some of the black students attended. They were well received. It was perhaps the quietest, most peaceful moment of their day.

Larry Taylor, Class of 1959

Some black students also had occasional opportunity to set aside their reserved composure, and in the company of appreciative white friends, assert their physical presence and personality with an energetic enthusiasm.

Bill McCauley and I enjoyed gym class with Terrence Roberts. Terrence was a brilliant young man who was obviously going to be successful in whatever career he chose. He was very tall, not well coordinated, but a tough basketball player. Bill and I always chose him for pickup basketball against a group of white long-haired "tuffs." We had great fun taking it to those guys when they tried to rough up Terrence ....

Wendell Ross, Class of 1959

No overt acts of heroism by white students were mentioned in the personal histories collected for this study. The closest to that was a description of how football player Bill Hicks spotted a person in the crowd at the June 1958 graduation program at Quigley Stadium. Hicks saw a package of eggs ready to be thrown at Ernest Green. He stopped that potentially inflammatory incident before it happened. Helen Ruth Smith Towns recalls Principal Matthews telling the students waiting to graduate that he would deny graduation to anyone who caused trouble that night.

Another minor incident of direct intervention was related by Paul Redditt, Class of 1960, who recalled a day in study hall when a black girl was repeatedly shot at with rubber bands by a white boy. Redditt wrote that a senior student seated in the very back of the room stood up, called the white boy by name, and told him to stop or he would be stopped. A brief shouting match ensued; the rubber band shooter sat down and sulked the rest of the hour.

Academic Assistance

Of all the things that have happened at Central, the most significant thing was the friendly attitude that students showed toward me the day of the rioting [Monday, September 23rd]. The type of thing that was going on outside, people beaten, cursed, the mob hysterics and all of this going on outside. We inside the school didn't realize the problems that were occurring and continually students were befriending us. I remember one case in particular in my physics class. I was three weeks behind in my assignments, and a couple of fellows offered to give me notes and to help me catch up the work that I had missed. I was amazed at this kind of attitude being shown toward the Negroes.[10]

Ernest Green, Class of 1958

At times, students assisted each other in their academic work without raising the attention or the ire of segregationists. Ernest Green, perhaps because he was the only senior among the Little Rock Nine, was identified in several student histories as a recipient of that help. Academic achievement, it should be remembered, was a point of pride for this group, so the opportunity to help a new student, particularly one who showed an interest and aptitude for advanced courses, was welcome.

In one student's history, she wrote about sharing her textbook for a week with Green until his personal copy was provided by the school. Another student, whose physics class preceded Green's, wrote about occasionally meeting with him during lunch to share her class notes and help him prepare in advance of the class.

I would try to help Ernest, either by clarifying an instruction we had been given or explaining some concept or telling him about an upcoming quiz or test. We talked infrequently and always about physics as I recall. Certainly our relationship was cordial, but never anything other than academic, two kids trying to get through high school physics with Mr. Barnes, who could be very difficult at times.

Glennys Oakes Johns, Class of 1958

Physics, a demanding class under normal conditions, must have been particularly challenging for Green, because he joined the class three weeks after it started. Green and the other black students did not begin classes at Central High until Monday, September 23, when they spent less than half a day in school because of the fear of mob violence outside. Two days later, with the 101st Airborne as their escort, their school year formally began. One of Green's physics lab partners shared the following memories about how two white students related to the late addition to their team:

The only senior in the Nine was Ernest Green. Ernest was always neatly dressed. He usually wore a white short-sleeved shirt and washed pants, green, of course. Placed in Mr. Barnes' physics class, Ernest's lab table assignment was with Charlie Oakley, a fellow trackster, and me. Ernest was quiet and polite. He was obviously uncomfortable and felt on display. I never heard any snide remarks or innuendo directed toward him or anyone else in physics class. We were all intent on performing the required tasks in physics so that we might somehow receive a passing grade and, yes, GRADUATE!

Mr. Barnes must have believed in learning by doing, since he sent us to the physics laboratory about four or five days a week. We were continually expected to assemble some type of experimental apparatus to demonstrate, presumably, certain scientific and/or physical phenomena. The result of this was that Charlie and I had some interaction with Ernest almost every day in physics lab. The instructions were difficult to comprehend. We prepared our lab procedures every night as well as we understood what the purpose of the next day's experiment would be.

Ernest was, understandably, behind because he joined the class late and he seemed to be finding the subject matter very difficult. Charlie and I never really discussed our actions, but it was just understood that we would attempt, whenever possible, to help Ernest assemble the experimental apparatus. Mr. Barnes usually wandered out of the lab after he took attendance. We freely discussed the experiments as we did them.

Tests were a different matter. Then it was every man for himself. We all passed.

Steve Swafford, Class of 1958

"Tiger" Articles and Editorials

The Central High newspaper, *The Tiger*, gave students a platform to express their views on events taking place at the school. Principal Matthews' column frequently offered a complimentary observation or expressed his pride on student behavior, following the educational model for positive reinforcement.

The newspaper content was subject to administrative review and editing. But a *Tiger* journalist, recalling her learning experiences at the school paper, had strong praise for the guidance of journalism instructor Edna Middlebrook.

How brilliantly Miss Middlebrook guided us in our writings for The Tiger. We didn't play down the situation, but certainly didn't glorify it, either. At the time, I didn't fully understand the term "power of the press" and grumbled that we were not able to write enough about events in and around the school. Now, I realize that we weren't so much being censored, as being shown a sense of proportion, and how to balance the news. Even now, I see <u>The Tiger</u> as a voice of reason in the midst of the chaos that was occurring outside the school.

Betty Ann Parsons Adams, Class of 1958

The student paper did not state a position on school desegregation. It did, however, repeatedly call for a moderate response by students to the social and political forces affecting the school. In an October 3 editorial, "The Price We Pay," the student editor wrote "No matter what our personal opinions may be, we cannot be proud of the violence that occurred around our school that made it necessary for the use of these federal troops. Looking back on this year will probably be with regret that integration could not have been accomplished peacefully, without incident, without publicity."

A second editorial that same day exhorted readers to "let the law take its course." Commenting on the crowds when school opened a month earlier, the paper described the street gathering as a "case of where a minority group controls the actions and even the thoughts of the majority."

Editorial writing at *The Tiger* was honored at the annual convention of the Arkansas High School Press Association in April 1958, when co-editors Georgia Dortch Sowers and Jane Emery Prather were named Editors of the Year. *The Tiger* staff also won individual awards for news, editorial, and column writing. Throughout the school year, stories and editorials from *The Tiger* had been quoted and re-printed in *The New York Times* and other national papers. On October 31, relatively early in the school year, Matthews wrote that Central High had already received thousands of letters from around the world, representing "viewpoints from the most violent segregationist to the most ardent integrationist" and a range of "mental attitude from the obviously insane fanatic to that of the highly intelligent philosopher." Matthews was encouraged by the many letters complimentary of the "sensible attitude of the student body." Apparently, some good news was getting out.

> To the editorial board of The Tiger: The student body of the Columbia University Graduate School of Journalism, including young people from all parts of this country and the world, commend the sane and courageous manner in which you have discussed rioting at Little Rock Central High. You have maintained a journalistic ideal of clear thinking under pressure. And we hope that your well and bravely voiced opinion will impress your readers and guide their behavior.
>
> Columbia School of Journalism

> Dear students: Even as a remote onlooker, I have been touched by your fortitude courage, and decency and take great pride and comfort in it .... You may wonder why I, a distant Northerner, even trouble to write you ... Simply because there are thousands who think and feel as I do—that every act of courage and decency is noticed and applauded by someone, somewhere, even if unknown to the doers. My respect and gratitude to you for having resisted engaging in any demagoguery or demonstrations.
>
> George Kartychok, New York City

In an era with fewer restraints than today on school-based expression of spiritual beliefs, Matthews was also impressed by a letter from what he called a young people's religious organization which commended the youth of Little Rock for their "dedication to the principles of Christian love and American democracy."

Letters to the school, particularly letters of international origin, received responses from the Pentangle Service Club, made up of two representatives from each of the five service clubs for junior and senior girls. The student club drafted a form letter of response, which included the comment, "Because reporters were not allowed in the school, there was little mention of the majority of the students, who objected to violence .... sought to continue their education .... conduct themselves properly and to accept the laws of our country."[11] [See Appendix E. Pentangle Service Board letter.]

As the school year neared its end, a May 8 editorial by Mike Barrier reminded students that the enrollment of nine black students had been projected to "scarcely jar the day to day routine" of the school's 1,950 white students.

"In a sense, they were right," Barrier wrote. "The Negroes have done little, in most cases, to draw attention to their actions. But early in the school year, a heated dispute arose over the actual entrance of the Negroes, and it has not yet abated .... The men of the 101st formed a stiff wall around the high school; their khaki-clad rigidity was in marked contrast to the exquisite boredom displayed by the National Guardsmen."

Barrier's description of the Arkansas National Guard may have reminded some students of *The Tiger* photos from the fall showing the state troops sleeping on the school lawn or posing for drawing classes as student sat outside with their sketch pads. The editorial concluded with a definitive statement of what Central High students had achieved throughout the year. "What has been in their power and will be, is the chance to display good citizenship and belief in law and order. Many people, including many northern correspondents, have expressed the view that Central's students have lived up to that chance."

Barrier's editorial is almost a statement of relief that the year was over and that nearly all Central High students had maintained a positive behavior. It only marginally alludes to the racial issues that remained unsettled, the complexity of what had happened in his school that year, and the larger historical significance of what it meant. His editorial respects Middlebrook's guidance to the staff not to glorify the events at Central High that year. He reminded readers that they had lived up to Brodie's statement of fact and challenge from September 25: "We will be, and are, good citizens."

A Policy of "No Discussion"

In the summer of 1957, the Capital Citizens' Council and the Mothers' League of Central High launched a media campaign against the Little Rock School Board's desegregation plan. Three years earlier when the plan was first conceived, it had gained a significant following, and in 1955, Superintendent Blossom had been named Citizen of the Year by the *Arkansas Democrat* for leading the city's compliance with the Supreme Court decisions. But as the opening of the 1957 school year came closer, the opposition became increasingly visible and strong. School officials decided the best response was to avoid confrontation at all costs. Since they believed discussion of the obviously volatile situation could quickly escalate into physical confrontation, all school discussion about it was prohibited inside Central High.

"Nor were students encouraged to discuss the explosive events going on around them. On the contrary, staff members commonly followed orders to stop discussion," wrote Graeme Cope. "A typical administrative bulletin intoned in September, 'This is a time of testing. The law and its interpretation we must leave to authorities charged with those duties. The less we discuss these matters the better'."[12]

Jane Emery Prather located in her memorabilia a copy of a September 4th bulletin sent by Principal Matthews to homeroom teachers. The bulletin, with instructions to teachers that it was to be read "without discussion in your homeroom," listed student responsibilities, including "quietly go about our business" and "refuse to be drawn into disputes or disputing groups." Matthews' advice was likely forgotten when a bomb threat caused all students and teachers to evacuate the building that same afternoon.

With daily events of such intensity occurring at the school, teachers sometimes utilized creative techniques to influence students, while following their principal's directive.

We had been told to keep the students away from the windows because no one knew what could happen. I saw the rabble's faces, heard their voices, and knew that education was not always just the ABC's. So I took my class to the library on the center of the third floor. When we were seated, I asked them to go one at a time to the pencil sharpener at the window and see the face of a mob. I told them that I wanted to forever burn in their minds what people look like who lose control of themselves and blindly follow the masses.

Elizabeth Riggs Brandon, English Teacher

Despite the policy of not discussing happenings with students, Industrial Arts instructor Paul Magro remembered how teachers relied on their students to keep them informed of daily happenings. On one occasion, history teacher Margaret Stewart dealt with an unexpected comment by Lloyd Erickson, who blurted out his wish that the adults would leave the school grounds. Erickson recalled that Stewart immediately ushered him into the hall where she agreed with him but reminded him of the "no discussion" policy. Erickson said he apologized and they returned to class.

Teachers informed us that our day was to be concentrated on study and learning rather than what was going on outside the school; we were not to go near the windows, we were not to discuss the issue of race or integration in the classroom or in gatherings in the hall, and we were not, when writing prose or poetry for class, to use this integration crisis as a topic. In my classes, the subject was taboo.

Helen Ruth Smith Towns, Class of 1958

The prohibition on classroom discussion or writing about race and integration was a security measure to avoid potential exploitation by segregationists. Similarly, school officials may have believed they would diminish chances of Central High's being shut down by the Governor, which was a real threat in everyone's mind, by canceling the planned student council-supported activity to welcome and orient the new black students.

Involvement of Student Leadership

> I was elected my homeroom's Student Council repre-
> sentative. Before school started, we were told to
> come to school for an important meeting. We learned
> there would be nine "colored" students attending and
> we were expected to show them around—help them
> find classrooms, lockers, the cafeteria, anything to
> make them welcome. I thought it was pretty cool and
> was more than willing to help. How naive I was.
>
> Roberta Martin Moore, Class of 1958

Central High Student Council officers had been elected in the spring of 1957 to serve a year term that would begin in September.[13] The group met several times during the summer with faculty sponsor Margaret Reiman. At every meeting, the officers discussed how the black students should be treated, and every time they agreed on what seemed a proper response: treat the new black students the same as new incoming white students. In mid-summer, the Council officers began planning a welcoming program for the incoming black students and all other new students after school started in the fall.

Late in August, Matthews decided to have an early registration and orientation for the black students on August 30. He asked the Student Council to serve as hosts for that event and include it in the welcoming program being planned. Not knowing the exact day that the black students would enter school, Vice Principal Elizabeth Huckaby personally prepared undated invitations for the Student Council to send to the Little Rock Nine.

Due to the uncertainty of the times, the planned event never happened. On the morning of August 30, Principal Matthews called it off because of potentially negative radio publicity, deciding instead that the black students would come to school on the opening day at the same time the white students came.[14] Probably a greater influence on the decision was the fact that senior Gail Blossom, the superintendent's daughter, had received a death threat over the phone the night before the planned event, prompting the last-minute cancellation.

The death threat was discussed in Gail's carpool some days later with speech teacher Shirley "Micky" McGalin Dunaway. Gail had been taught to be polite to all callers, and her cheery response to the intimidation, "Thank you for calling," was spoken without a second thought, Dunaway said.

But cheerfulness could not overcome the real threat of danger. The Student Council kept its planned Welcoming Program on hold for four weeks until Friday, September 27, when Matthews informed them the event was again cancelled for safety reasons.

The risk to anyone who participated in such a program was clear. After the second cancellation, no meeting with the Little Rock Nine was discussed or planned again by the Student Council officers. Had such a program taken place, student leaders might have developed personal impressions of the black students, and even more importantly, might have assumed some personal responsibility for them as individuals. Instead, like the rest of the student body, they began the school year with no advance opportunity to learn the personalities or backgrounds of the nine black students.

The Troublemakers

We had our share of troublemakers inside the building, but troublemakers will always find a reason to cause trouble, whether or not they are the subject of a national media showcase.

Carolyn Glover Hirby, Class of 1960

There were a few individual students, possibly encouraged by their parents, who acted out and caused some incidents as pro-segregationists. However, from my own observations and the comments of my father [Principal Matthews], I knew these students were few and far between that year.

Joe Matthews, Class of 1958

Like most schools, Central High had a small, unorganized rough group of students identified by their wearing of leather jackets and the smoking of cigarettes. Most had little interest in education or were bored with typical school activities. This estrangement alone does not categorize them as bullies or disruptive sorts. But within this group were an active few who utilized the desegregation issue to express their anti-social position.

At Central High in 1957, these students were more commonly found in the sophomore and junior classes. At that age, they may have been more easily influenced by organized adult backing from staunch segregationists outside the school. According to Cope, the small number of seniors in this group of discontents suggests that seniors more commonly displayed the pragmatism evident among so many Central High pupils: "...with an eye to graduation, most seniors knuckled down to work and made the best of what they took to be a raw deal..."[15]

Students who displayed active opposition to integration were usually neither high achievers nor pupils prominent among homeroom officeholders, sportsmen, cheerleaders, members of Student Council, Key Club, National Honor Society, Beta Club, or musicians and budding thespians. Not one of the fifty-one females who succeeded in first tryouts for cheerleader in March 1958 was a publicly-declared segregationist. Typically, few segregationists worked on the yearbook or the twice-monthly student newspaper, *The Tiger*. None of the school's hostesses and community fund-raisers, the Southernaires and Debonaires, gave any indication of opposition to integration."[16]

Who were the troublemakers, and what had they been doing before desegregation put them in the spotlight?

The answer can partially be found in the memoirs of Andrew Young, later mayor of Atlanta and U.S. ambassador to the United Nations, who in 1957 was a staff member of the National Council of Churches located in New York. That fall, Young was sent to Little Rock to meet with local ministers in the Little Rock Council of Churches who were looking for ways to calm the situation at Central High.

"In our analysis of the problem," Young wrote in *An Easy Burden*, "we discovered that the kids involved in the violent incidents at the school were by and large those with a history of causing other kinds of trouble. And none of the mainline churches had any contact with these unruly teens through any of their youth programs.

"We began to meet with school officials to persuade them that they didn't have an integration problem: they had a discipline problem. The usual troublemakers were getting support from adults who opposed integration, but basically they were the same kids who disrupted the classrooms and broke rules before integration began. With the real issues properly identified, local churches looked for ways to build bridges and help the kids in Little Rock understand the reasons for desegregation."[17]

Problem Students

> Many of the white students who were disruptive were the same "problem" students from the year before; the difference was that now they had encouragement and approval from adults on the outside in their harassment of the black students. They handed out hate literature, and a few were relentless in their efforts to disrupt. I remember telling my homeroom students regularly, "Don't do anything today that you can't live with the rest of your life."[18]
>
> Shirley Swaim Stancil, Guidance Counselor

All students who attended Central High on a daily basis and applied themselves to their school tasks displayed a quality of courage. They routinely experienced distractions and intimidations inside and outside the building, not the least of which were forty-six bomb scares, many of which required the building to be evacuated and all lockers searched. Superintendent Blossom has suggested that of the 1,963 students enrolled at Central that year, the "great majority acted with dignity and tact."

> Most of the students, I would say 95 percent, accepted the Negro pupils quietly and with dignity. During the

51

year, the student body displayed an attitude of good sense and good citizenship, with the exception of a small hard core of segregationist-minded boys and girls. These never numbered more than twenty-five or possibly fifty, and they were a small minority compared to the other students, many of whom went out of their way to make the Negroes welcome."[19]

Virgil Blossom, Little Rock Schools Superintendent

The opportunity for teenage pranks, even among well-behaved students, should not be overlooked. Some of the student foolishness simply challenged authority.

Another student and I raised the U.S. and state flags each morning at reveille. The flag poles were at the fish pond in front of the school. The 101st was bivouacked all around the area and each morning would be assembled in front of the school. They were usually standing around at a military status of "at ease," meaning they could stand in place in a relaxed position.

The instant the U.S. flag was clipped onto the lines, the troops would be required to come to a "parade rest" status per military protocol. This means standing motionless, with feet slightly separated, hands clasped together behind your back, and head facing straight forward. The soldier might possibly move his eyes a little, but for the most part, a parade rest position is a motionless position.

So, it was not too long until we decided to get to school exceedingly early in the mornings, get the flag clipped on the pole, and see just how long we could keep these guys standing motionless at the parade rest position.

52

After a couple mornings of them standing there for at least thirty to forty-five minutes, the troops quickly noticed that we were doing this purposely, just to antagonize them. So they blocked us from getting the flag from the office each morning until about five minutes before reveille. Oh well, what youngsters will do for entertainment! It seemed the entire year that we students would think up ways to antagonize the troops, and they would retaliate in some way or the other. None of it was done out of anger or hate, but simply being kids, and having fun.

Ralph M. Brink, Sr., Class of 1958

Other incidents of student pranks, as evidenced by the story below, became the stimulus for more abusive activity and exploitation.

One night I went over to a friend's house and we made a dummy out of a black sock, some straw, a sweatshirt and a pair of old blue jeans. The plan was to take it up the stairs and hang it out of Central's band tower. It was just a couple of kids pulling a stupid prank. We got the "effigy" to school, but we chickened out and left the dummy in the third floor restroom.

The next day the TV screens and newspapers were full of the most outlandish stories about the effigy. Within a couple of weeks, our dummy was featured in *Life*, *Look*, *Newsweek* and several other magazines. It seems some other students found the effigy and managed to get it across the street from the school. They hung it out of a tree and some of the bystanders attempted to set fire to it. One student told me that some of the reporters on the scene were lending

students their cigarette lighters to light the effigy.
Looking back, this was not a smart move on our part.
It just gave fuel to the media frenzy.

Paul Barnes, Class of 1958

Historians and school officials have tried to put a head count on
the "small minority" Blossom mentioned. During the school year,
305 incidents of student segregationist activities led to disciplinary
action. Within this number, 181 were for individual acts of passive
resistance, such as sign-outs and walkouts which did not involve any
contact or harassment of the Little Rock Nine. Most of the 181 student walkouts happened on two days: September 25, when the Little
Rock Nine first entered Central High under federal protection, and
on October 3, when the Mothers' League sponsored a walkout. These
passive actions generally earned the participating student a three-day
suspension and did not involve the Little Rock Nine in any way.

However, school records identify 124 incidents, including acts of
verbal abuse or physical harassment, directly involving the Little Rock
Nine.[20] Court records reveal that approximately 5 percent of Central
High students (eighty-seven out of 1,963) caused the problems, with
about twenty-five students acting as ringleaders.[21] Cope wrote that
according to "one of the most extreme segregationists," these problem
students, didn't bother with all "that stuff" from teachers about behav-
ing properly.[22] They were pupils who, by stalking out of school and
actively abusing the Little Rock Nine, both verbally and physically,
attracted disproportionate attention, intimidated helpful whites, and
tarnished the reputation of the Central High student body as a whole.

Limited Sanctions on Problem Students

After an earlier incident in which Minnijean Brown
"accidentally" stumbled and spilled her chili on a
couple of students who regularly heckled her,
Minnijean was moved to our lunch period, and she
began eating with the other black students at the end
of our table. One day some students, as I recall maybe

54

two boys, dumped a bowl of soup on Minnie's head. That was horrible.

The lunch room erupted. Kids all around us were clamoring up on top of the tables, yelling and screaming, raising their arms and stamping their feet to cheer. I was acutely aware that I, my friends, and those black students were at the center of a near riot. I knew that if one of those tables fell over or a leg failed, we would be beaten and severely harmed, even killed by a mob. These were students that I saw every day, was acquainted with many of them, and yet on that day, they were a mob.

Fortunately, the soldiers entered the lunch room quickly, the black students were safely removed, and order was restored. I went home from school that day shaken and scared. The next day, I ate lunch with my usual group, both white and black. It was the only day that I was really frightened.

Glennys Oakes Johns, Class of 1958

The frightening lunchroom incidents reflect a concerted effort by problem students to find the most volatile personality among the black students and push that person to a point of breakdown. School officials, ever wary of the opportunity for false accusations, had implemented a policy requiring an adult witness to any reports of harassment. For black students, this was tantamount to an open door for intolerant white students clever enough to avoid detection. For most white students, the policy reduced their chances of witnessing or reporting those covert acts.

The harassment that did take place—the stalking and bullying, the defacement of property, the physical contact—is unacceptable in any decent society, as it was unacceptable to most Central High students then. Efforts would have been made by capable students to stop such conduct if it occurred in their presence. Student leaders, including Key Club and football team members who had been alerted by Principal

Matthews early in the school year. They were told their help might be needed with problem people from outside. But as the year progressed, the student leaders were repeatedly being told that the problem inside Central was under control. The students assumed school discipline was being as rigidly enforced as it had been in previous years and authorities were correcting whatever problems occurred.

> Our experience in prior years was that discipline, once handed out by our principal and vice principals, was severe enough that the offender's conduct was radically changed. If not, his or her days were soon spent in other places outside of Central High. We expected no less during 1957-58. We were unaware, however, that school discipline was not being rigorously enforced by our principals that year as it had been in all previous years and that the conduct of the problem students was not responding as expected.
>
> Ralph Brodie, Class of 1958

In the case of Minnijean Brown Trickey, the bullying students broke through the composure that the other Little Rock Nine had maintained through the year. The incident described above took place in December and brought short-term suspensions to Trickey and the white students involved. The attacks on Trickey continued following her return to school. In February 1958, she had reached her limit. The fourth and final confrontation between her and a white student, when she admittedly used the term "white trash," resulted in her expulsion from Central High. The white student received only a suspension. Shortly afterwards, a few white students handed out and sported lapel cards that read, "One down…Eight to go." The offensive cards were confiscated, and additional students were expelled. But a bad precedent had been set, and irrevocable damage had been done.

The failure to expel students whose conduct deserved that result, who were constantly in disciplinary trouble, was harmful not only to the safety of the Little Rock Nine but also to the morale of the faculty and other students who openly supported them.

In 1957-58, the school's policy of "don't talk about it, don't publicize it," kept many students and community members uninformed and strengthened the resolve of the segregationist opposition. For this policy, Matthews was publicly criticized by the local chapter of the NAACP, which accused him of failing to use sufficiently harsh disciplinary measures against offending white students.[23] A year later, this strategy did not convince Little Rock voters to keep the school open.

Media Truth and Distortions

> My mother was watching national television coverage from her home in west Little Rock. The reporter was making it sound like a riot was happening. Mother called the school to advise me to leave immediately for my own safety. At the same time, I was watching the same commotion out my window at 13th and Park across from Central, and nothing was happening.
>
> Pat New Graves, Class of 1958

In 1950, televisions were found in only five percent of U.S. homes.[24] By 1957, however, eighty percent of the homes in the United States owned TVs. When President Eisenhower went on national television on September 24, 1957 to explain his decision to intervene in the Central High crisis, an audience of one hundred million people, representing sixty-two percent of the nation's television sets, was tuned to him. Television coverage of the 101st Airborne Division's first full day in Little Rock was watched in the Pentagon by Army Secretary Wilbur Brucker and his Chief of Staff Maxwell D. Taylor, who noted with a military displeasure that the belt of one federal soldier was undone.[25]

At Central High, the street crowds quickly realized the capacity of the media to convey their presence and their message to a national audience. But, as the media message uniformly showed them in a negative light, the mob began to assault and abuse reporters and cameramen. David Halberstam wrote that "reporters were at risk all the time for the mobs perceived them as liberals, Jews, and communists."[26] Black reporter Alex Wilson was attacked on the street, and white newsmen were harassed. The media responded with an increasingly simplistic perspective. It focused on Little Rock white citizens, and correspondingly, white students from Central High who, from their own inclination or for the benefit of the media, were willing to express or act out racist beliefs.

> According to newspapers and TV commentators, most white students were out of control redneck racists, to the point of running wild in the streets outside school, screaming at the police, the Arkansas National Guard, and the black children. Also according to them, fights and race riots were common inside our school and race hatred raged among the students and throughout the general population in the city, events that would be hard to miss, but not one of which I saw that year.
>
> Art Pearrow, Class of 1958

There was strong competition among them to capture on film the events unfolding before them. The sense of competition resulted in payments to locals in exchange for photographic poses. In an affidavit dated May 1998, James V. Stahlkopf, an adult cameraman for KARK-TV Channel 4 in Little Rock from 1956 to 1958, states:

> On two occasions, I personally witnessed and filmed out-of-state reporters/photographers actually making monetary payments to students/young people. I later observed one of the young people/students who was paid by these reporters throw objects at officials escorting the Negro students into the school. It was clear that these payments were being made to encourage the students/young people to stage certain events so that the reporters/photographers could get

58

pictures of a racial incident for their story/TV report on the Little Rock situation.

James V. Stahlkopf

Several student stories describe a situation they witnessed of students being paid to pose for photographs or take action.

A reporter offered three kids $20 each to pose throwing rocks. I was the fourth, but three of them each got a $20 bill to pose for the picture. They couldn't find any rocks over there. There weren't any rocks on the campus, and there weren't any rocks across the street over there. And they broke some pieces of bark off a tree that was in the yard across the street from school, and the three boys had big chunks of bark in their hand, not rocks. They took some pictures, and I watched that. His name was Frank McGee, and he had a photographer with him. He wasn't taking the pictures; he was just directing the action.

Phil Filiatreau, Class of 1958

That second day in 1957, I watched reporters in the crowd give boys $10 bills to start a fight. They did, too. I watched them run a block from the crowd, jump on an old black man with a cane, hobbling along. He was so old, he didn't even know what was going on. They got their pictures and they were in the news all over the nation the next day. The reporters were from Time magazine and other out-of-town respectable sources. Just a boy in the crowd, I saw it all. A friend who worked at Channel 4 told me they got $1,000, maybe $2,000 for each photo. They made their own news for money.

Student Name Withheld

Will Counts' dramatic photos captured the moment when Elizabeth Eckford was turned away from Central High by the Arkansas National Guard. His photos follow her as she walked to a nearby bus bench and waited in stoic silence with the raging mob around her.

Counts was fortunate to be in the right place at the right time. CBS News television and radio reporter Robert Schakne was not. His cameraman was too late to film the contorted faces and the yelling. By now, the crowd was standing about the bench. The action had ended.

A chapter in *The Race Beat*, a Pulitzer Prize-winning book focusing on media and civil rights, explains that Schakne, realizing what his cameraman had missed, did what many enterprising media reporters of the time might do. He ordered up an artificial retake.

He urged the crowd, which had fallen quieter, to demonstrate its anger again, this time for the cameras. "Yell again," Schakne implored, as his cameraman started filming. Suddenly the lawn at Central High had become the set, the television reporter had become the director, and the demonstrators had become his actors. Schakne was re-creating news; that moment was a clear chance for a whole new round of demonstration and gesticulation.[27]

Schakne's violation of media ethics is far less common in 2007 than it was fifty years ago. But at the time, the opportunity seemed clear. A highly inflammatory crowd scene had just occurred. For the TV journalists on hand, capturing the truth of that scene through a camera was the primary objective. In the 1950s, re-creating the events seemed to them a perfectly viable way to tell that truth.

To be newsworthy you had to spit, throw soup, or call someone a derogatory name. The media had a preconceived notion of how students felt and sought out the few students who confirmed that notion. The antics of Sammie Dean Parker were portrayed as typical of the entire student body.

Students were also baited to perform. Two football players were approached by someone claiming to be a reporter for <u>Time</u> magazine and offered $25 each to hit a black student. The only stipulation was that the attack had to be done outside where it could be filmed.

Ron Deal, Class of 1959

One day in the girls' locker room, one of the girls came in late laughing and waving around what was a pretty good-sized handful of money. She was excited because a reporter from a nationwide magazine had stopped to talk to a group of students and told them things were too quiet. He wanted them to pose for a picture walking in front of a soldier with a weapon pointed at them. She took him up on it and was paid $75.

Margaret Johnson Swaty, Class of 1958

The photo for which the girls were paid appeared on page one of the September 25 *Arkansas Democrat* and was circulated worldwide the next day. Its caption stated: "Dispersal order—Students who declined to enter Central High but attempted to remain as spectators were hurried away by bayonets of soldiers on duty at the school." The image shows two students, apparently laughing, as they walk away from soldiers whose bayoneted weapons are pointed at their backs. The posed photo shoot was witnessed by Gaylon Boshears, a 1957 Central High graduate who had joined the Army and was home on leave from basic training. That morning, a member of the 101st allowed Boshears to cross the guarded perimeter of the school, giving him a close view of the incident.

"Nothing about this picture was true," Boshears said. "I saw someone bring the soldiers and the students to that location to pose for the photographer."

Other photographers, as well, had opportunity to stage news. Early in the crisis, the crowd had not yet learned how its belligerent voice and gestures would be negatively portrayed by national media. Indeed, reporters were unsparing in their portrayals of the hundreds of sign-toting chanting white opponents of desegregation who gathered in front of the school every morning. They were described as shabby, ragged, trashy, unshaven men and frowzy women, riffraff, truculent street corner drunks, the viragos of the back alley tenements, the squatters on near forgotten Tobacco Roads.[28] Once this media bias was recognized, the crowd turned its anger on the journalists.

Benjamin Fine, the *New York Times* reporter who briefly consoled Eckford as she sat on the bus stop bench, found himself the target of such emotions. Trying to interview white teenagers after Eckford departed, Fine was circled by a crowd. A National Guard lieutenant colonel ordered him to stop. Other newsmen gathered around, and around them was a crowd of whites who jeered and taunted the newsmen as they were herded toward Major General Sherman Clinger, the Governor's appointee as Adjutant General in charge of the National Guard. Clinger told Fine he would be arrested if it seemed in the judgment of the troop commander that he was inciting to violence.[29]

After Art Pearrow graduated from Central High in 1958, he worked as a news photographer for Little Rock's KATV Channel 7 for nine years during the 1960s. During that time, media personnel talked freely about their conduct as if the integration of Central High had been a game.

I believe that members of the national and local news media openly and intentionally distorted the stories about Central High with staged events, pictures, and misleading commentary based on those distortions. They did what they did to get more air time, thus more recognition, when the real story and actions didn't justify being on national TV. Once these stories were aired, journalists could not recant what they had done. To do so would be to tell the world that they were at fault and had caused a serious misrepresentation of the truth. This would make all of us, the viewing audience in America, ask what else has been reported in this manner?

One of my favorite quotes came from an older local news person I got to know in the 1960s. He would often say: "Never let the facts get in the way of a good story."

Art Pearrow, Class of 1958

Intentional distortions by news media have been a problem for Central High students and teachers since these staged events were documented for historical purposes. Further, these filmed images are part of the archives of the event that have been studied by researchers for decades. The truth behind many of these false images has never been fully disclosed.

Finally, the willingness of some news media to print unverified information and juxtapose it alongside a completely contradictory story must be recognized. In this case, the *Arkansas Democrat* on Monday, September 23 published two front page stories. The headline of one account, written by a staff reporter, proclaimed "Growing Violence Forces Withdrawal of 8 Negro Students at Central High." In the next column, a story by the Associated Press was titled "Nothing Much Happened."

The local reporter quoted a white student who said fights broke out inside the school after the black students entered the building, blacks were chased through the hallways, and they had blood on their clothing. The Associated Press reporter quoted two of the Little Rock Nine. Terrence Roberts said, "Nothing really happened…There was not a whole lot of trouble. I was pushed but I don't know anybody that got hit." And Thelma Mothershed said, "Nothing much happened. I went to three classes. There was no shouting or anything."

Media complacency about verifying information, particularly sensationalist accounts that promote false understanding, is not balanced by simply printing an alternate and truthful version of the events. The local article left readers with the clear impression that violence had occurred inside Central High. The damage had been done.

Ira Lipman and John Chancellor

During the Central High confrontation, NBC's John Chancellor, provided highly credible and objective reporting of events. Chancellor's effective work at Central High was made possible by his relationship with student Ira Lipman.

As a junior, Lipman attended Central High, but he transferred to Hall High for his senior year with others members of his debate team. The team coach, Marguerite Metcalf, had chosen to work at the new

63

high school, and she asked the four-student team if they would follow and keep the team intact. At Hall, Lipman became the business manager of the student newspaper and yearbook. The newspaper was printed on the presses at Central High. Bringing ad copy to the school print room, Lipman had access to Central High on a daily basis. In the evenings, he also worked part-time at the *Arkansas Gazette*, reporting state high school football results.

The two activities made Lipman a perfect contact for NBC newsman Frank McGee, who asked Lipman to help arrange an interview with students to express their views on integration.

> That Sunday, September 8, 1957, I participated in a panel discussion with fourteen other students, filmed in front of Central High School. On live television, I declared that the American people "must obey the law of the land." The Arkansas Gazette reported the event on the next day's front page, without naming the students. Within one hour of the broadcast, my family had received telephone threats against my life. My mother and my 10-year-old sister, Carol, each answered separate phone calls. Carol was shocked when she heard the person on the other line say that he wanted to kill me.
>
> Ira Lipman, Hall High Class of 1958

Lipman's involvement is included in *The Race Beat*. The book tells that Lipman followed the televised program by writing a letter to Jewish youth leaders across the nation, seeking their support for forcing Faubus to comply with the law. He urged them to stand up and play a role in bringing change.[30]

A month later, Lipman sent birthday greetings to President Eisenhower to let him know he had student support. Lipman received a reply from the President that stated, "I am grateful to you and your fellow high school students in Little Rock for your message of good wishes on my birthday anniversary, ... It is gratifying to me to have your re-affirmation of one of the basic beliefs of all Americans—respect for the law of the land."[31]

Lipman's most significant role, however, came after Frank McGee left Little Rock and John Chancellor took his place. Chancellor contacted Lipman and asked his help as a news source. The request gave Lipman a reason to contact Ernest Green, whom he knew because Green had worked as a locker room attendant at the Jewish country club in southwest Little Rock where the Lipman family were members.

With information from Green passed through Lipman, Chancellor was the only reporter on hand when the black students entered Central High through a side door on Monday, September 23. At Lipman's request, Green also agreed to respond to Chancellor's brief questions. Chancellor's exemplary work, much of it assisted by Lipman's continuing tips and inside information, set a new standard for television reporting.[32]

Voices From Central High: Mike Wallace Interview With Ralph Brodie

On the first day of school, September 3, 1957, Mike Wallace, then a reporter with the *New York Post* and ABC TV, later of *Sixty Minutes* fame, telephoned the principal's office at Central High and requested to talk to the student body president. Ralph Brodie was summoned promptly. At the time, neither Brodie nor Vice Principal for Girls Elizabeth Huckaby, who was present and hovered with concern, had any idea who Mike Wallace was.

Brodie recalls being puzzled (who was this reporter and what was the purpose for his questions?), but he tried to answer him politely and truthfully. After a few moments, it became evident that by using leading questions, Wallace was trying to elicit sensational and racist comments. When the questions stopped and phone interview was over, Brodie turned to Huckaby and said, "That man was trying to make us all look bad!"

After this interview was published, the quality of the responses the 17-year old Brodie maintained during his phone interview were rewarded with a letter of commendation from Adolphine Terry, who later founded the Women's Emergency Committee in the fall of 1958 when the schools were closed. Brodie said that after the interview's publication two weeks later his Arkansas relatives, who lived outside Little Rock, feared for his life.

Originally published in the column, "Mike Wallace Asks" in the *New York Post*, the interview was reprinted in the *Arkansas Gazette* September 17, 1957. On September 19, an editorial by Jane Emery Prather titled "Can You Meet the Challenge?" was published in *The Tiger*. The editorial asked students to display their maturity and intelligence through proper decisions and conduct that showed respect for the law.

67

Within a week of publication, the Little Rock Nine made their first entry into the school, the most serious confrontations at Central High had begun, and the presence of the 101st had turned school building and grounds into an armed camp. The clear voices of these two student leaders may have been overwhelmed by the maelstrom that followed, but the values they so clearly expressed were exhibited in the behavior of most of the students.

The Wallace-Brodie interview on the first day of school is presented here in its entirety.

Wallace: Ralph, as president of the student body at Central High School in Little Rock, how do you feel about the situation down there? Are you alarmed about it?

Brodie: I'm not.

Wallace: Why has all this tension been brought to bear down there?

Brodie: I think you can read the papers and find that out.

Wallace: Are the people in your town upset about troops [Arkansas National Guard] being called in? Did this upset you?

Brodie: I didn't care for it. I'll put it that way

Wallace: Do you think there will be any violence?

Brodie: No, I don't. We are praying there won't.

Wallace: How long do you think this tension is going to last?

Brodie: That's up to Governor Faubus.

Wallace: If you had your say, speaking personally, the Negro students could come to school tomorrow?

Brodie: Sir, it's the law. We are going to have to face it some time.

Wallace: Do you think the day is going to come when your school is going to be integrated?

Brodie: Yes.

Wallace: Are you opposed to integration yourself?
Brodie: If it's a court order, we have to follow it and abide by the law.

Wallace: Would you mind sitting next to a Negro in school?
Brodie: No.

Wallace: How does the student body feel?
Brodie: Pro and con.

Wallace: Have there been any meetings among the students?
Brodie: No, there haven't. It hasn't been felt there was any need of such.

Wallace: Would you say the sentiment is mostly toward integration or segregation?
Brodie: I really don't know just how to answer that.

Wallace: You can't ....
Brodie: We are going to have integration some time, so we might as well have it now.

Wallace: Do you think there will be much resistance among students when this day comes around?
Brodie: I don't believe there will be any at all.

Wallace: That's interesting—then there is a big difference in the way your age group feels about the race problem and the way your parents feel?
Brodie: I don't know just how to answer that question. I think we just better skip that.

Wallace: Do you have any Negro friends?
Brodie: No, sir.

Wallace: Have you done any soul-searching at all about the segregation problem as a whole?
Brodie: Not particularly.

69

Wallace: Would it make a big difference to you if you saw a white girl dating a Negro boy?
Brodie: I believe it would.

Wallace: It would?
Brodie: Yes, sir.

Wallace: Why?
Brodie: I don't know. I was just brought up that way.

Wallace: Do you think Negroes are equal in intelligence and physically to white people?
Brodie: That is just a matter of opinion.

Wallace: What is yours? You are a person of some significance; you are president of the student body.
Brodie: If they have had the same benefits and advantages, I think they're equally as smart.

Wallace: Do you respect the Supreme Court?
Brodie: I certainly do.

Wallace: Do you believe all Southerners should live by the law of the land?
Brodie: I don't see why we shouldn't. We've been living under it all of our lives.

Excerpts of the *New York Post* were reprinted as courtesy of the *New York Post*.

Chapter 2

Arkansas and the South

Understanding Southern Rhetoric

I was born in McRae, Arkansas [a town fifty miles north of Little Rock] which was a "sundown town," meaning no black person was to be there after sundown. There was a sign on each side of town at the city limits warning black people. I never asked if it was a city ordinance or a group of people making this town rule.

I was never taught in school or at home to hate or look down on black people or anyone else. I was never around any black people except to see them when we went to Beebe, and I never knew of any mistreatment to them except to see the signs at all restrooms and eating places and their places were all in the back. I don't remember ever having any feelings toward them one way or another. It was just accepted in those days as the way it was supposed to be.

Charles Evans Forte, Class of 1958

"I am a segregationist," wrote Wayne Upton, president of the Little Rock School Board in October 1957. "I steadfastly refuse to be drawn into an integrationist versus segregationist controversy."[33]

Another school board member, Henry Rath, stated his position just as clearly, writing, "I am in accord with the contents of Mr. Wayne Upton's letter. I am a segregationist."[34]

These statements seem shocking today. But the terms "segrega-tionist," "integrationist," and "moderate" must be understood in the 1957 context when they dominated public conversation about school desegregation efforts.

At that time, the two school board members were responding to "The Little Rock Story," a two-part article that appeared October 7 and 8 in the *Arkansas Democrat*. The writer, New York-based Relman Morin of the Associated Press, had interviewed Superintendent Blossom for his story. Morin was told that Upton and Rath were vic-tors in a recent school board election, having defeated candidates with extreme segregationist positions. Morin, erroneously assuming Upton and Rath held opposite positions, labeled the men as integrationists in his article. Upon its publication, Upton and Rath immediately wrote to Morin, who quickly apologized for his misunderstanding.[35]

The polite exchange between the men and the content of their direct statements may be misleading. Upton was an attorney; Rath was a treasurer with a local bakery. Both men were respected in the community and considered moderates, if not liberals. With the con-cept of segregation having been held unconstitutional when applied to public education, why did these school board members, both mod-els of moderation, label themselves as segregationists?

Upton's letter offers insight into this terminology. In his school board election campaign, Upton had publicly approved the limited and gradual plan of integration adopted by the Little Rock School Board in 1955, but beyond that he took no public stand on the issue. For Upton, the election simply meant a choice on the part of people between "compliance with the law and defiance of the law."[36] Upton campaigned and won on the concept of compliance. He subordinat-ed his personal views to the law of the land. The law, for him, had greater value than his personal feelings.

A similar dynamic was being played out on the highest levels of the federal government. President Dwight D. Eisenhower also subor-dinated his personal feelings in favor of enforcement of law. In a per-sonal interview in October 1957, the President said he believed the Supreme Court decision was wrong because it should have focused on equal opportunities rather than on absolute equal integration. On the Court's ruling that separate education facilities were inherently unequal, Eisenhower responded, "I am thoroughly familiar with that argument, but I do not find it compelling."[37]

In the context of the time, "segregation" reflected the practices and values of a social system developed fifty years earlier under the assumption that white supremacy was moral and right and would last forever.[38] For white people in both the North and the South, these assumptions would not die quickly; nor would they be easily unwound. "Segregation" meant maintaining the status quo by law and by force if necessary. A "moderate" position would reluctantly accept some social change letting it take its natural course, while an "integrationist" view would approve of accelerated change and intervention, if necessary.

> Like a multitude of other Southern white young people, I was very happy with the status quo. It was just how life was. I never really thought about how it was for black people. I assumed that their schools were like ours, but they just went there and we went to our schools.
>
> Dorothy Hawn Larch, Class of 1959

To challenge that social system, as "integration" did, was to undermine a pillar of Southern and American civilization. "Integration," as a result of its court-required introduction into public education, was a radical change forced upon the people and unwelcomed by most Southern whites except a small group of visionary liberals and reformists. Additionally, "integration" raised the taboo specter of race-mixing, a highly inflammatory concept for most Southerners. Being a "moderate" was a middle-ground position opposed by segregationists, because it allowed change, and by integrationists, because it would not allow for change to occur rapidly.

> I never heard any white adults say they were supportive of integration. Responsible adults might say conditions for blacks should be improved, but the practice of segregation was not questioned. Instead,

73

the most liberal view would be that segregation would have to change—but slowly. The implication that I recall hearing from adults, especially teachers, was that the courts or the national government was forcing integration upon the state or the South.

Jane Emery Prather, Class of 1958

Today, our terminology, as it applies to public education, views "segregation" as morally wrong and "integration" as ethically superior. For the majority of whites in America in 1957, segregation was the favored way of life. Many Central High students and faculty were personally opposed to desegregation. Because of that view, their good conduct and their belief in the "rule of law" deserve respect. Beyond the terminology of "desegregation," "integration," or "segregation," Central High insiders accepted their responsibilities as professional educators, good students, and law-abiding citizens.

Some of my close friends would call me an integrationist. Not a nice word at the time. And during the discussion they would always say "Well, are you going to marry a black?" That was what an integrationist was to them. They would always quote the Bible to me also. I lost many friends that year because of being an "integrationist."

Mary Ann Rath Marion, Class of 1959

Integration and Communism

In his book *The Fifties*, David Halberstam wrote that during the early 1950s "McCarthyism crystallized and politicized the anxieties of a nation living in a dangerous new era. He took people who were at the worst guilty of political naiveté and accused them of treason. He set out to do the unthinkable, and it turned out to be surprisingly thinkable." McCarthy charged that our control of events was limited because sinister forces, i.e., "communist sympathizers in the government," were at work against us. The problem with America, he was saying, was domestic subversion, as tolerated and encouraged by the Democratic Party. His point was simple: The Democrats were "soft on communism."[39] With that often-repeated message, he fanned the fear of Communism within American politics for decades to come.

Segregationists were quick to draw a connection between integration and Communism. In the Arkansas gubernatorial campaign of 1956, Governor Faubus' primary opponent was extremist James D. Johnson, who charged Faubus with being "soft on integration," merely another version of "soft on Communism" as the desegregation efforts were equated time and again with Communism in extremists' circles. Integration, they declared, was a denial of individual rights, a law forced upon them by a distant totalitarian government. In addition, integration was widely denounced as being part of the Communist effort to destroy America by stirring up racial unrest to undermine the social fabric of the South.

The perceived threat of Communism to the American identity as a champion of individual liberty was acknowledged by President Eisenhower in his September 24 televised remarks regarding the assignment of federal troops to Little Rock. After explaining what the 101st Airborne would and would not do at Central High, Eisenhower said, "At a time when we face grave situations abroad because of the hatred that Communism bears towards a system of government based on human rights, it would be difficult to exaggerate the harm that is being done to the prestige and influence and indeed to the safety of our nation and the world. Our enemies are gloating over this incident and using it everywhere to misrepresent our whole nation. We are portrayed as a violator of those standards which the peoples of the world united to proclaim in the charter of the United Nations."[40]

Southern Response:
Massive Resistance and the Southern Manifesto

My mother had a few choice words about the stupidity of the U.S. President, whom she did not like anyway because he was a Republican. She was also an extreme

Southern segregationist and did not like the
interference of anybody in what she felt was no one's
business but the City of Little Rock and the State of
Arkansas.

Alice Harper Curtis Dixon, Class of 1958

Except for President Truman's 1947 Executive Order integrating
the armed forces and the U.S. Supreme Court's 1954 decision in
Brown vs. Board of Education, no branch of the federal government had
done much to further black civil rights since the 1869 passage of the
Fifteenth Amendment which guaranteed blacks the right to vote.
After the Supreme Court's 1954 decision, battle lines in the South
were quickly drawn as Southern politicians were confronted with the
racial issues that enveloped much of the nation. The crisis over
emerging black civil rights posed no dilemma for most Southern
politicians. They were unalterably opposed to them.

All but a notable handful of politicians demagogued the issue and
planned a campaign known as "Massive Resistance," a term coined by
Senator Harry Byrd of Virginia.[41] The campaign included the theory
of state sovereignty, which rejected the authority of the Supreme
Court to interpose its will between that of the people and their state
government. White Southern legislators and school boards enacted
pupil assignment laws and created other strategies designed to avoid
compliance with the Supreme Court's mandate in *Brown*. Newly
formed White Citizens' Councils were created in all southern states
to counter the Court's integration decision.

Northern states' strategies to ensure segregation of the races
included the creation of new, smaller school districts drawn purposely along racial lines. In the South, the campaign also included writing
the Southern Manifesto. Authored by a group of Southern congressmen, the Southern Manifesto denounced federal encroachment on
the states. In 1956, nearly every congressman in the Deep South, 101
in total, including Arkansas' six congressmen and two senators, signed
it.[42] Calling the *Brown* decision "a clear abuse of judicial power," the
Southern Manifesto stated:

76

We decry the Supreme Court's encroachments on rights reserved to the States and to the people, contrary to established law and to the Constitution...

We commend the motives of those States which have declared the intention to resist forced integration by any lawful means...

We pledge ourselves to use all lawful means to bring about a reversal of this decision which is contrary to the Constitution and to prevent the use of force in its implementation.[43]

An additional political gauntlet had been thrown down by several Southern governors who threatened to close their states' public schools if desegregation were mandated. Governor Marvin Griffin of Georgia repeated his threats in Little Rock in late August only days before school started in 1957.

Griffin had won his state's Democratic gubernatorial nomination in September 1954 with a campaign pledge that "come hell or high water, races will not be mixed in Georgia schools."[44] In August 1957, he delivered a similar message to the Capital Citizens' Council at Little Rock, where he said he would call out the National Guard to prevent integration in his state. Commenting a year later on the speech, Griffin said, "If it stiffened opposition to integration, then I have no apology to make to anyone."[45]

Not all Southern governors were as adamant as Griffin. North Carolina's Luther Hodges respected the law enough to accept an unpopular decision. After state court decisions prohibited action to prevent black people from entering the schools of three North Carolina cities, Hodges said, "The state and the people of North Carolina will not tolerate any lawlessness or violence."[46]

Arkansas' Position

Integration was foreign to the majority of the people in the South, and most people were content to live the way we had lived for decades. White children attended all white schools, and black children attended all black schools. Neighborhoods and churches were segregated. We were creatures of habit and tradition that were established long before our time—and no one was rocking the boat!

Carolyn Glover Hirby, Class of 1960

If a Southern role model existed for racial progress, Arkansas could have been it before 1957. A moderate state, as much Southwestern as it was truly Southern, Arkansas' medical and law schools had been integrated in 1948. Republican and Democratic state committees had black members before those in any other Southern state. Several towns had proceeded with desegregation of their public schools, including Fayetteville, Bentonville, Charleston, Hot Springs, Fort Smith, and Hoxie. In Little Rock, the public bus service, library, parks, and zoo were desegregated.

Governor Orval Faubus, considered a moderate in 1955, spoke of the good will that existed between the races and that had made Arkansas "a model for other Southern states in all matters affecting the relationship between the races."[47]

Nevertheless, Faubus promised voters in 1956 that no Arkansas school district would be forced to mix the races as long as he was governor. He supported several initiated acts favoring segregation that were passed by the legislature in early 1957. This set of laws authorized the governor to close desegregated public schools and transfer their assets and tax income to private academies. Additional segregation laws were passed, including one that allowed parents to refuse to send their students to integrated schools. Supporters of segregation, including Griffin and other Southern governors, pressed Faubus to join them and openly resist integration.[48]

Faubus' choices brought world attention to Little Rock and rapidly changed Arkansas' identity as a moderate state. Faubus' political leadership played to the prejudices of the people. A different style of leadership, statesmanship rather than demagoguery, might have brought different results. Progressive changes in Little Rock and other Arkansas cities showed that its citizens would obey the law and not openly defy it. But Arkansans, like most Southerners, detested federal interference with their schools.

School Board Decisions and Community Response

Like the summer rainstorms which pelted the city every afternoon, other thunderstorms loomed on the horizons of Little Rock in the late summer of 1957. There was talk of "integrating" Central High. Tempers ran high; newspaper headlines shouted about this and that. I strongly felt that if any student wanted an education, he or she deserved the best that any community could provide. It seemed that my father and grandmother disagreed. These were sentiments which I never before dreamed they had held. The atmosphere thickened, subtle tensions rose, unspoken beliefs surfaced, and national attention became focused on this obscure town called "Little Rock."

As the beginning of the school year approached, tensions mounted, and by the first day of school, the city was in turmoil. These diametrically opposed political and moral conflicts split apart not only the town but also individual families. Mine was one. The dinner table was more silent than usual, punctuated only by "Pass the potatoes, please." and "May I be excused?"

One afternoon, a circulating petition protesting the integration of Central High was brought to our front porch. My grandmother and father signed it. I asked to read it and then tore it up. The silence became black. I regretted that act, knowing intellectually that it was wrong, but my emotions had become raw also.

Yvonne Thompson, Class of 1958

79

In May 1954, five days after the Supreme Court's decision in *Brown* declared segregated schools unconstitutional, the Little Rock School Board voted to end its dual school system. By 1955, the Board had adopted a plan to desegregate the city schools in stages, starting with Central High in 1957. All six members of the Board approved the "Blossom Plan" despite their opposition to integration. They had been assured by the Board's attorneys that it represented a legal minimum of compliance with the law.[49]

The Board's original plan was to begin at the lower levels and work upward, on the theory that younger children would have learned less prejudice. But Superintendent Blossom found that parental fear was more intense concerning lower grades than secondary levels. Parents were less nervous about their teenagers than their first-graders.

In May 1955, with *Brown II* requiring "all deliberate speed," the Board adopted a phased-in integration plan for Little Rock to begin at Central High and take six years to reach the first grade. The school board planned to operate four high schools that year, each serving a unique demographic group: Central High was a school for middle- and working-class whites; Hall High was a new suburban school in the rapidly growing and predominantly white northwest wealthier part of town; Horace Mann was the black high school; and Little Rock Vo-Tech was a white technical school.

Integration was scheduled to begin at Central High, while Hall High was to open as an all-white school and receive black students the next year as part of the phased-in plan. If city leaders saw this as a double standard, they seemed untroubled by it.[50] Overall, the community seemed to take it in stride, but there were some who resented the decision.

Moderate white leadership in Little Rock was not strongly opposed to school desegregation. As businessmen, they understood that a fight to maintain white supremacy would be self-defeating. They accepted the idea of desegregation, but they remained wary of social equality. At the heart of their position was the desire to do business as usual. The presence of a white redneck mob in the street was a much greater threat to tranquility and daily commerce than was the desegregation of the public school system. Hamilton Moses, president of Arkansas Power & Light, appalled at the thought of widespread racial trouble, told *Arkansas Gazette* Editor Harry Ashmore, "If the Klan starts riding again we'll never sell another bond on Wall Street."[51]

> For some time my dad [Little Rock Mayor Woodrow Mann] had been in a series of strategy and planning sessions with both city and school officials, preparing for the court-ordered integration of Central High. According to him, the majority opinion of those in charge was that they expected the opening of Central to go relatively smoothly.
>
> Woody Mann, Class of 1958

The desegregation process began with a list of eighty students from the all-black Horace Mann High School whose families were willing to consider the new approach. School officials reduced that to thirty-two students, eliminating those not ready for the social pressure or the schoolwork. Additional families dropped out when they learned that, because of safety concerns, black students would not be allowed to participate in athletics or other public-attended, extracurricular activities, such as band or chorus. The list shrank from seventeen names to a final group of ten, and one more dropped out after Elizabeth Eckford's September 4th encounter with the National Guard and the mob. The students chose Central High primarily because the school offered a stronger college preparatory curriculum than the black high school. All nine were planning to go to college.

Forces Arrayed against Central High

> We didn't have any friends or associates that were black. We lived completely separate. I can remember very well the water fountains in the downtown department stores, Blass, Pfeifers, and all those. You had a white restroom and you had a colored restroom, as they called it then. They had a water fountain for whites, and they had a water fountain for colored.

81

Most restaurants had a back room or a room on the
other side where the colored could go in and eat.

Phil Filiatreau, Class of 1958

Woodrow Mann was elected mayor of Little Rock, his native city,
in 1955. A reformer, he installed a newly integrated bus system, condemned the city's purchasing agency, and launched numerous inves-
tigative committees within six months. He overturned Jim Crow
rules that forced blacks to use cups at the City Hall water fountains,
doubled the number of black policemen from two to four, and inves-
tigated integrating the fire department, whose chief said white fire-
fighters would not sleep in the same room as blacks.

Mann may have over-estimated the willingness of city agencies
and personnel to accept his changes. After less than a year, Mann's
reforms and other political problems provoked a referendum in the
spring of 1957, changing Little Rock's government to a city
council/city manager system, in effect making Mann a lame duck.

Tensions were clearly mounting as the city drew closer to the
start-up date of the school board's desegregation plan. The spring
1957 school board election was, according to Superintendent
Blossom, "a vicious campaign in which the segregationist organization fired its heavy guns, but the citizens in the city rallied enthusias-
tically behind Upton and Rath and scored a smashing two-to-one tri-
umph, indicating a powerful moderate majority in the city."[52]

Blossom believed the segregationists had been defeated in
attempts to turn the people of Little Rock away from respect for the
law of the land. He was confident the phase-in program would go
smoothly at the opening of the 1957 school year.

Opposing this position was the Mothers' League of Central High,
which organized and held its first public meetings in late August
1957.[53] The Mothers' League and its sponsor, the Capital Citizens'
Council, were the only organized groups openly opposed to desegregation. Creation of the Mothers' League by the Citizens' Council was
an attempt to soften the face of virulent racism by linking the segregationist cause to the sacred and emotional strengths of Christianity
and Southern motherhood.

82

I had grown up with all the prejudiced assumptions of
my environment. But I had also been exposed to the
influence of the church. My family were devout
Christians. And there was this argument within me
between what my society and my church taught me in
story and song, but not in example.

Larry Taylor, Class of 1959

Both the Mothers' League and the Citizens' Council had additional influence inside Central High through their children who were students at the school. The Mothers' League size was estimated at greater than 160 members, but membership required only an expressed commitment to the segregationist position. There were no dues, regularly convened meetings, or newsletters. Thirty-three women in the Mothers' League were parents of children at Central High. Among the 500 members of the Capital Citizens' Council, only five had children at Central High.[54]

School Board President Wayne Upton called the Mothers' League "just an irritant…a thorn in the side."[55] But the Mothers' League was involved in multiple activities opposing desegregation, including court actions, active participation in crowds outside Central High, and sponsorship of a student walkout on October 3. On October 4, more than 200 women rallied at the Governor's mansion, calling on him to close the school. In a November 1957 letter sent to all Central High parents, the League called desegregation efforts "a conspiracy of evil forces confronting free men."

The rhetoric of the Mothers' League took its cue from Citizens' Council literature, which commonly noted that white leaders who followed the Supreme Court's ruling had "bowed the neck and bent the knee" to federal authority.[56] In a highly self-righteous and melodramatic tone, the Mothers' League letter asserted that "divine providence" had delivered the conflict to Little Rock and urged its readers: "We must awaken, arouse, and alert those who do not as yet understand the wickedness of those forces arrayed against us. The control of our schools, the education of our children, the sanctity and dignity of human freedom—everything that free men hold dear is in the process of being gradually taken away from us."

All Deliberate Speed

Before the start of the 1957-58 school year, at a general teachers meeting held at West Side Junior High School, Superintendent Blossom announced the impending enrollment of black students at Central High. Blossom spoke of a second Supreme Court ruling, known as *Brown II* of 1955, which set out the Court's vague time table to begin the desegregation process. Paul Magro, an industrial arts teacher at Central High, recalled Blossom's explaining the Court's term "with all deliberate speed," which identified the issues that could be considered when creating a desegregation plan, and the intent of the Little Rock School Board to begin desegregation that school year.

> Those of us on the faculty knew that our responsibility at Central was to make it all work, it was our job to do, and we did a good job of it. But nobody except those of us who were there wants to acknowledge that fact.
>
> Faculty Name Withheld

Events did move quickly that fall following the Governor's removal of the Arkansas National Guard at Central High. After Friday, September 20, the city police became responsible for crowd control. The mobs at Central High began their planned disruption. On Monday morning, September 23, the day the Little Rock Nine entered Central High through a side door, the crowd out front was engaged in violence against four black newsmen. Once the black students were inside, several white students climbed out of windows and screamed "They're in, the n**** are in."

Outside the school, the crowd moved against the police lines, and rocks and bottles began flying at passing cars. Protesters yelled to the children inside the school, demanding that they come out. They cheered those students who came out; they also cheered a police officer who turned in his badge. Assistant Chief of Police Gene Smith said he was able to keep his men on the security line at the school only by keeping a gun to the backs of their heads.[57] Mayor Mann's request to Fire Chief Gann Nalley to use hoses on the mob was ignored.

Whites attacked reporters and cameramen, and newsmen were thrown in the police wagon along with assailants.[58]

At mid-morning, city police realized the situation could escalate beyond their control, and they took the black students home. By noon, Central High had been re-segregated, and calm returned.

Photos of the mob violence by Will Counts, particularly the beating of black journalist Alex Wilson, reached President Eisenhower, who reportedly said, "I've got to do something."[59] Impatient for assistance, Mayor Mann took matters into his own hands and telegraphed President Eisenhower with the following message:

Telegram to President, [Tuesday] September 24, 1957—The immediate need for federal troops is urgent. The mob is much larger in numbers at 8 a.m. than any time yesterday. People are converging on the scene from all directions. Mob is armed and engaging in fisticuffs and others acts of violence. Situation is out of control and police cannot disperse the mob. I am pleading to you as President of the United States in the interest of humanity, law and order, and because of democracy worldwide to provide the necessary federal troops within several hours. Action by you will restore peace and order and compliance with your proclamation.—Woodrow Wilson Mann, Mayor of Little Rock, Arkansas[60]

That evening, Eisenhower made his televised statement about the deployment of the 101st Airborne Division to Little Rock. A thousand riot-trained soldiers arrived in Little Rock the same evening, clearly indicating a state of readiness. Future Arkansas governor Frank White, on his first mission flying a C-130, was one of the Air Force pilots who delivered the "Screaming Eagles" to Little Rock that evening.[61]

The Politics of Governor Orval Faubus

He could have chosen the high road and provided leadership to the people of Arkansas by demanding we obey the law of the land, regardless of our personal feelings. Instead, he chose the low road—the road of self-aggrandizement. He appealed to the worst elements in our nature. He created the crisis. By predicting violence he legitimatized it. All of this happened because Orval Faubus chose the low road.

Lloyd Erickson, Class of 1958

When Faubus spoke on television on Monday night, September 2, he informed the citizens of Arkansas that he had instructed the state National Guard to fulfill his constitutional duty to maintain order at Central High. He said Arkansas was handling race relations quite well, but federal courts were ignoring the public wishes and usurping the state's authority, a process that would bring about widespread disorder and violence. "It will not be possible to restore and maintain order and protect the lives and property of the citizens," Faubus said, "if forcible integration is carried out tomorrow in the schools of this community."

Faubus had given few indications that he would deploy the National Guard. With little publicity, he met with Griffin, the segregationist governor of Georgia, and Roy Harris, overall head of the Citizens' Councils, after Griffin's speech on August 22 at Little Rock. The two men stayed at the Governor's Mansion and had breakfast with Faubus. The liberal moderate camp saw the visit as a turning point, the moment when Faubus looked at his political future, saw no middle ground, and made his choice.[62]

But Faubus had been weighing his options for some time. Since 1955, he had utilized the polling organization Mid-South Opinion Surveys to learn the state's position on school integration. Surveys showed that eighty-five percent of the people interviewed across the state were against immediate integration. In September 1957,

Eugene Newsom, owner of the polling firm, was asked by the Governor to find out what the people thought about the imminence of violence if the schools were integrated and what they thought about the governor calling out the National Guard to prevent disorder. It is unknown if Newsom's survey distinguished how the National Guard might be used: as crowd control or to bar black student entry to schools. Predictably, the survey showed whites overwhelmingly in favor of the Governor calling out the National Guard units. The survey showed that blacks, on the other hand, were nearly unanimous in their belief that little or no disorder would occur if the National Guard were not called out.[63]

Earlier that spring, the package of segregationist bills endorsed by Faubus passed through the Legislature by near unanimous votes. Although the laws would prove to be invalid in the confrontation that soon developed between the federal and state powers, Faubus was responding to the growing pressure for segregationist policies and was positioning himself as a symbol of Southern white resistance. Foremost in the Governor's mind was probably his own political future. In Arkansas, a governor ran for reelection every two years, and Arkansas voters were notoriously ungenerous about handing out third terms. Faubus was not a lawyer and had no assurance of a staff position at one of Little Rock's prestigious law firms. He had no family wealth to fall back on, and he did not look forward to going back to being a rural postmaster or small town newspaper publisher.[64]

So Faubus must have felt confident that his televised remarks on September 2 would be believed and strengthen his political future. He described Little Rock stores selling out their stocks of knives to black youths and a large number of revolvers taken from high school students. Police reports never substantiated the Governor's statements, and Faubus never kept his promise to reveal the evidence he cited.[65]

History has not been kind to the man at the center of this storm. Many believe he deserves no kindness, that his opportunistic decision was achieved at enormous cost to countless others and with deliberate disregard for the disruption and trauma he introduced in their lives.

Was Faubus the calculating Machiavellian who, as McCarthy did earlier, intentionally politicized racial anxieties and new social realities? Or was he "a small man from the hills," as Fulbright described him,[66] a victim of his own weakness, who betrayed his conscience and intelligence for the sake of political expediency, a man who knew better but couldn't do it?[67]

A tragic hero, in the classical definition, must inspire pity and awe. The tragic hero demonstrates admirable qualities, but in the end, personal weaknesses destroy him. On Sophocles' or Shakespeare's stage, that weakness is hubris or pride. Faubus' stage was the white marble halls of the Arkansas statehouse, where, in a defining self-centered moment, he responded to questions that he had abandoned his promise to Eisenhower of a compromise solution, saying, "Just because I said it, doesn't make it so."[68]

Removal of the National Guard

For seventeen days, Faubus claimed that his placement of the National Guard at Central High was to preserve peace and maintain order. On September 20, he decided differently. His removal of the National Guard from its Central High assignment affirmed his own predictions of violence. Effectively abandoning both black and white students to the mob, Faubus claimed he, too, like the entire state of Arkansas, was subject to the forced intervention of the courts.

In a 1991 booklet called "The Faubus Years," the former Arkansas Governor offered this explanation and defense of his actions:

> I have always felt, and still firmly believe, that if the school authorities in Little Rock had handled the affair quietly, the intense conflict over integration at Central High would never have developed. If the school authorities had said, "This is our own local problem. We'll handle it the best we can based on our local conditions. This does not concern any other school. Just us." If they had said that and the media had followed that lead, there would have been no Central High School Crisis as we now know it.

Although crowds gathered, everything was peaceful with the few National Guardsmen in control. In the course of events a federal judge, at the request of the Justice Department, ordered me to remove the National Guard. I promptly complied with the order.

Evidence suggests that these remarks attempt a self-vindicating revisionism. As a result of Faubus' interference, Little Rock school authorities were in no position to "handle the affair quietly." Further, the federal court order did not order him to remove the National Guard. The order said Faubus was "enjoined and restrained" from "(a) obstructing or preventing...(b) from threatening or coercing...or (c) from obstructing or interfering with the constitutional right of the Negro children to attend said school..."[69]

Faubus' response, the removal of the National Guard, has been the subject of extensive interpretation. His lifelong insistence that he was ordered to remove the National Guard has created a pervasive acceptance of this falsehood. The language of the court order identified only one change in the use of the National Guard; it could no longer be used to block the black students' attendance. The order contained no suggestion on how to use the National Guard other than restating the governor's authority to use the Guard to preserve the peace.

Faubus adapted the court order to his personal gain. *Arkansas Democrat-Gazette* Editor Paul Greenberg, a 1969 Pulitzer Prize winner for editorial writing, suggests that Faubus, when challenged to uphold the law, used the opportunity to get around the law, outwit federal and state governance, and get himself re-elected.[70] He did so by activating the violence he had predicted. Rather than redirect the National Guard to enforce crowd control and assist the enrollment of the Little Rock Nine, a move that might have redeemed him in history's eyes, Faubus used the court order as an excuse to remove the National Guard troops. In so doing, he abandoned his constitutional obligation to preserve peace and order. It was his last chance to do the right thing, a chance he traded off for a vainglorious moment of self-justification.

In the years that followed the 1957 Little Rock school crisis, Faubus utilized the Arkansas State Police as a political arm for the governor's office to conduct surveillance and investigation of political foes, blacks and "left-wingers," and others.[71] When his sixth term in office ended in 1965, his fortunes took a downturn. By the close of his life in 1994, he had suffered several personal tragedies and lived on meager resources in Conway, Arkansas.

Voices From Central High: On the School Grounds

I remember a few of the white students being on the sidewalk outside the school shouting up to us in the windows, "Come on out. You don't want to go to school with n****s." I did not come out. I did not want to be out there in the mob.

Avay Gray Jaynes, Class of 1960

Vividly I remember a particular day in gym class. We dressed out in gym gear and went out back to play softball. Army helicopters, military jeeps and equipment, and hundreds of uniformed soldiers were sharing our playing field. It was so unreal. The two worlds didn't fit together. My 18-year old eyes were used to dealing with nothing more important than what I was going to wear tomorrow and trying to memorize 100 lines of "The Rime of the Ancient Mariner" for Miss Mary Piercey's class. And there we were, surrounded by men, some not much older than we were, with bayonets fixed on rifles with orders to protect us and our school building even if it meant blood might run in the streets around Central.

Sandra Buck Palmer, Class of 1958

On our way across campus, we saw a girl climbing out of one of the classroom windows, and I wondered, "What's with her?" We learned from the crowd that she was Sammie Dean Parker, and when one of the Nine showed up in her home room, she bailed out the window.

Barbara Jo Norman Griffis, Class of 1959

By late August, tension in the city was almost unbearable. Angry racists threatened to picket Central High. A confrontation appeared inevitable. The first day of school [Tuesday, September 3], I saw Arkansas National Guardsmen in full battle uniform standing shoulder-to-shoulder at parade rest. Wooden barricades blocked streets. No traffic moved anywhere at Central High School. Already a large crowd of people had gathered.

The first day the Little Rock Nine entered the building [Monday, September 23], word circulated inside the school, and the building erupted with noise. Bedlam broke out. Students left classes and roamed the halls. A couple of students in my study hall bolted from their seats to join the revelers in the halls.

Larry Taylor, Class of 1959

On September 23, the crowd had begun to gather at the south end of Park Street and the police were trying to hold them back. I could see this from the window in a first floor room. The crowd began to move toward the police and the police line wavered, fell back, but rallied and met the crowd head on. I saw one sergeant run to his police car, open the trunk, and fumble for his tear gas rifle. He appeared to be very apprehensive. The police arrested a few people and placed them in a police car. The police are to be commended for handling a very explosive situation that first day as well as they did.

Wednesday morning the 25, I left home and walked to Central High. At 14th and Summit Street, I was stopped by some paratroopers. Some of the streets about three blocks from school were blocked. I had to show my pass before I was permitted to continue to school. The soldiers were all in full force, with bayonets at the ready. I had not seen or carried a bayonet since the last battle on Okinawa. Those troops meant business. They were everywhere. They set up a command post at the football stadium. I saw rifle marksmen stationed on the roof of Central High.

Paul Magro, Industrial Arts Teacher

Suddenly the streets leading to the school were barricaded, and we had to walk two or three blocks to get to the building. There were 101st Airborne personnel with guns strategically located throughout the school monitoring the change of classes. In Alberta Harris' speech and drama class located on the stage, teaching frequently came to a stand-still because of the noise of helicopters taking off and landing in the football practice field located just behind the auditorium stage.

Jo Ellen Clark Barnard, Class of 1958

Chapter 3

The Consequences

The Students

My boyfriend said, "Are you going in that school?" I said, "Yes. Aren't you?" He said, "Hell, no, and I'm not going steady with any n**** lover." With that, he jerked his high school ring from around my neck and walked away. I was shocked and brokenhearted. I could see there was going to be a price paid for making the decision to graduate at Central High.

Sherrie Smith Oldham, Class of 1958

Among Central High's 1,950 students in 1957, nine black students made a deliberate and courageous choice to challenge a defined social order. They were unmistakable targets when the storm of consequences came upon them.

We had to endure rowdy mobs of adults blocking the streets and hostile mobs of students who opposed integration blocking the stairs and halls, pushing, jostling, and shouting obscenities.

These words are not a black student talking. They are part of the memories of Yvonne Thompson, a white student at Central High. Thompson recalled being pelted by the mob with eggs and tomatoes as she and others helped black students enter the building on September 23. She also recalled an afternoon when students hid under their desks to escape rocks, bricks, and broken glass when the windows of her first floor debate class were targeted by the mob.

95

Thompson is part of a larger group of students and staff who experienced the school desegregation crisis in uniquely personal ways. An understanding of how some white people were also affected by the malicious actions of their peers should elicit no comparison to the experiences of black people, the Little Rock Nine, or any other group. This is not a competition in suffering.

Rather, a study of the consequences experienced by many people shows the commonality of the core event, its broad impact on the community, and the process by which our eyes are opened to social injustices that have, in some cases, been accepted as a part of life.

> Our country is better and stronger because of integration, but I think that the price was paid by many—both black and white. Families were broken up to provide a senior year, college scholarships were lost, businesses were damaged, and our city still bears a shame that was not all of our making. It would be wrong to ignore the hundreds of Central High students and their families who made an effort to set a standard of kindness and normalcy during that turbulent time. This was a grand experiment for them, also.
>
> Elizabeth Riggs Brandon, English Teacher

The consequences of taking a stand against racial injustice were well known to black Arkansans long before the events of 1957. They had always lived in a world where horrific violence had been inflicted on those who overstepped the lines of social order or who were innocent victims of mob violence.

Thirty years earlier, Little Rock's last lynching was a 1927 nightmare event that included a public burning of the black man's corpse. An unresolved murder and corpse-burning occurred in 1954 in Marion County in east Arkansas, followed by the nationally publicized death of Emmett Till in Mississippi in 1955.

Scenarios of extreme racial violence are permanently fixed in the landscape of the Southern mind. In the traditional pattern, whites inflict it and blacks receive it. That pattern is challenged, however, when white people who assist or befriend blacks are persecuted by other whites. For a young black person whose only experience has been traditional racial roles, the new understanding can dramatically change his or her world view. Elizabeth Eckford had such a moment, but it wasn't until 1996 when she learned of the consequences paid by two white students with whom she'd become friends.

> One girl named Ann Williams Wedaman lived on a farm outside the city, and her father had to hire armed guards for their home. And the other student is Ken Reinhardt. Ken was harassed. He'd been knocked down, one time, he said, right in front of the gym teacher and the gym teacher did nothing.[72]
>
> Elizabeth Eckford, Class of 1959

Over the school year, Reinhardt experienced much more than this single incident. The student who knocked him down in gym class was a persistent tormentor, Reinhardt said, who on the very last day of school punched him in the face during another gym class. Because he and the attacking student had essentially graduated from school, no discipline action was taken at that late date.

Reinhardt recalled a last encounter with the student the following year when both were attending Ouachita Baptist University in Arkadelphia, Arkansas. Passing each other on campus, the student nodded a silent acknowledgement to Reinhardt and walked on. His restraint on that occasion, Reinhardt believed, was indicative of the college atmosphere where such personal attacks would not be tolerated.

At Central High, Reinhardt's overt gestures of friendship with Eckford and other black students resulted in numerous threats against him and anonymous calls to his parents, as well as alienation from some classmates. Many incidents of reprisal against whites occurred throughout the school year, possibly as part of what some school officials suspected to be a calculated campaign organized out of the governor's mansion. Such maltreatment was also noted in *The Fifties*, where Halberstam commented that systematic and extremely well-organized harassment was more effec-

97

tively carried out on any white child who was courteous and friendly to the black children.[73]

Reinhardt, who in recent years has joined Eckford in public speaking programs, reminds his audiences that the actions against black students were far more aggressive than those he or other whites received. But more significant than Halberstam's and Reinhardt's comparisons of which group may have had it worse is the result of those experiences on both groups. The positive value of these experiences is the compassion created between black and white students who realized they both were receiving cruel treatment by a bullying group of people and how that realization made them treat others better.

For some white students, such as Central High's cheerleader squads, the consequences were not dramatic. Helen Ruth Smith Towns, captain for the varsity cheerleaders, recalled her group was prohibited from leading cheers that including the word "black," even though black and gold were the school colors. "Yea Gold, Yea Black, Yea Tigers, Push 'em back" was dropped at the request of Helen Hazel, cheerleader faculty sponsor, who believed the cheer could be offensive to the black students and a potential trigger for a disturbance. But groups from other schools still jeered at the Central High students when football games were played at Quigley Stadium.

> Students from other schools heckled us. After games played at Central, the students would lean out their bus and car windows and shout, "Two, four, six, eight, we don't have to integrate." At first we found them annoying, but later we just laughed at them.
>
> Helen Ruth Smith Towns, Class of 1958

At football games with the 101st Airborne in attendance, Central High students sometimes responded to derogatory anti-integration cheers with lighthearted, impromptu calls of their own, such as "Three, five, seven, nine, the 101st has changed my mind." But most consequences were more serious than cheers or jeers. The reprisals included forty-six bomb threats throughout the year, which often required building evacuations in the guise of fire drills so that Central

High coaches could check student lockers. That task was later assigned to the soldiers of the 101st Airborne Division, who noisily banged open the lockers with the base of their rifles while teachers in nearby classes attempted to ignore the clamor.

Some parents were very protective that year. Many of them needed to be.

> The hatred that gathered on those streets was the fear of change and prejudice toward a person that was different. That hatred could be, and in some cases was, acted out on the white child who dared to cross the line to attend the school of their choice.
>
> Sherrie Smith Oldham, Class of 1958

Brodie said he learned thirty years later that his father had rebuffed an FBI agent who asked about Ralph's becoming a student informant inside Central High. The agent was angrily admonished by the senior Brodie never to contact Ralph. Other forms of endangerment of white students who had friendly relations with blacks included painting obscenities on that person's locker, as Margaret Johnson Swaty said was done to her locker numerous times. In the cafeteria, students surrounded her, grabbed her lunch tray, and threw it away. When the act was repeated on subsequent days, Swaty began going to the Campus Inn snack bar for lunch.

> Melba Patillo and I walked down the halls at times together after Chapel. If we went the same way more than once, there were students who would be taunting. I could handle name-calling, but to this day I am afraid of being pushed and shoved both up and down stairs and always use the wall side of a set of stairs.
>
> Margaret Johnson Swaty, Class of 1958

The possibility of physical harm was real. Barbara Barnes Broce, another student at Chapel, had developed a casual friendship with Ernest Green. One morning in the hallway outside Chapel, they were

99

approached by a group Broce called the "black jackets," meaning they wore the leather jackets of motorcycle riders and affected a tough attitude. Taunting names were spoken behind her back. When Broce turned, both she and Green were pushed against the lockers, kicked, and harassed. Green ran off as soon as the attack ended, she said.

> I was stunned, but I can vividly remember that I felt abandoned. Why in the world would he walk beside me, and talk with me, and be my friend and then run off? Later, Ernest told me that any time a black student was in any altercation of any kind, they had been instructed to go to the principal's office when that occurred.
>
> Barbara Barnes Broce, Class of 1958

Central High students were challenged to convince the world they were not the radicals being portrayed to the nation. They did this through acts of friendship toward the Little Rock Nine. Those same acts inflamed the radicals outside and inside the school doors and gave them a directed target for their campaigns.

> Did the students really learn anything that year? Of course they learned something, probably not all that they could have, but a great deal did not come from a textbook. The students whose parents were screaming the loudest about segregated schools were learning more prejudice and hatred. The "good students" were also learning some of life's more unpleasant but important lessons about truth and honesty and what too much political ambition can do to some individuals.
>
> Carol Ann Lackey Patterson, Typing Teacher

The lessons learned by students often went beyond what their parents could teach them. Lynn Weber Sigmund saw her experiences at Central High as the "beginning of my journey toward becoming

100

outspoken" and as a catalyst for her understanding of how children can evolve beyond their parents' experiences.

> My father was a segregationist, but he and my mother understood they were raised in a different time and often said they wanted us to be better persons than they. I also want that for my children.
>
> Lynn Weber Sigmund, Class of 1958

Threats to Families

> My mother told me she received a phone call from an anonymous person who said I had been eating lunch with black students. Since the event never happened, I was always curious about who might have made the call, and why.
>
> Jo Ellen Clark Barnard, Class of 1958

The chaotic events that marked the opening of the school year in September 1957 subsided as the weeks and months passed. By Thanksgiving, the 101st Airborne Division had been removed, and the federalized Arkansas National Guard, while continuing to provide security oversight to the school, had shifted to a much less visible role. The battlefield that was Central High had settled into distinct strategic positions. Nine black students were attending the school and would continue to do so if the situation were left alone. Little Rock's phased-in desegregation plan would be fulfilled unless something was done to disrupt it.

Before the end of 1957, the city prosecuting attorney's office found little public support for punitive measures, and local judges dismissed charges against those arrested for disturbances outside Central High. Emboldened by the sentiment of the times, extreme segregationists stepped up their threats and campaigns of harassment. While they were unable to stop the desegregation process at its start, they were determined to make life hell for all those involved. The object was to panic the parents of white Central High students and destroy the credibility of the administration.[74]

On March 7, 1958, Blossom's wife received a call from an unidentified male who threatened her husband's life. On March 8, Blossom heard a shot when he was within two blocks of his home. The next day he found evidence which indicated his car had been hit by a bullet.[75]

The families of many Central High students were not spared intimidation. Jane Emery Prather said abusive phone calls to her mother and hate mail to her home began arriving immediately after Jane agreed to walk beside Ernest Green in the baccalaureate and graduation services.

> My father had died the previous summer, adding to my mother's anxiety, as she felt very much alone. The incident had a profound effect on me. I was so angry at these racist and hateful people. I was determined that I had to leave the South for college.
>
> Jane Emery Prather, Class of 1958

The callers commonly expressed their anger and threatened reprisals for white students sitting with blacks during lunch or attending morning worship services together in the Chapel Club.

> A lot of adults outside the school didn't like blacks and whites mixing for worship in Central High's chapel. My parents received threatening phone calls that cursed and called us who attended Chapel names, threatening our family if I didn't quit going to chapel. My parents continued getting calls all that school year, all hours of the night, in which they would only hear loud breathing—not a word said.
>
> Margaret Johnson Swaty, Class of 1958

Seniors Joe Matthews and Woody Mann remember numerous calls that suggested the students, their homes, or their parents would be targeted. Police cars often were stationed outside their homes. On the morning of September 6, Mayor Mann, often quoted in the *Arkansas Gazette* as opposing Faubus' deployment of the National Guard, found a cross burning in his yard. The following evening, Lloyd Erickson was walking a familiar path between the houses of his midtown neighborhood.

As I was walking over to Woody's, I was hit by a police spotlight and asked in no uncertain terms to identify myself. This repeated itself many times over the next several weeks. How sad it was that someone who was simply trying to obey the law would have to have police protection.

Lloyd Erickson, Class of 1958

Mary Ann Rath Marion remembers being bumped in the halls and accused of being a n**** lover because she had befriended one of the blacks. She was the daughter of school board member Henry Rath, the financial officer at a local bakery, who learned of a boycott against his company. Early in the school year, a Rath family outing gave ominous clues to the difficult year ahead.

One morning Mother was packing a picnic lunch for all of us, including Daddy. We were going to miss school and Daddy was going to miss work and there was nothing wrong with any of us! What was going on? That evening we were told there were several bomb threats against us and it was better for us not to have gone to school that day. After that, there was always a car parked down the block watching us.

Mary Ann Rath Marion, Class of 1959

The threats to the students and families caused strong parental concern. In the summer before the school year started, threats were received by black families after a newspaper listed the names of their children who had applied to attend Central High. Within that group,

Melba Patillo's mother, a teacher in North Little Rock, lost her job because of her daughter's participation.

The rock that shattered Daisy Bates' home window carried the note, "Stone this time. Dynamite next time." The rock that broke the window of Central High teacher Susie West's apartment was tied with a paper note, "N****-loving bitch." And though the rock that came through student Jane Teague Allred's home windows carried no note, its message was clear enough for the family to keep the drapes closed on the front of the house. Following numerous threatening phone calls, her parents joined with others and hired private detectives to follow the students to school and school functions, she said.

Parental influence on the children was strong at that time. Barbara Barnes Broce was prohibited by her mother from responding to national media that asked for the student's comments on activity inside Central High. Broce recalled her mother's fear of the injuries her daughter might receive following such an interview.

But not all adolescents take their parents' advice or share their concerns, particularly when the issue involves an idealistic belief.

> One time my mother called me at school and begged me to skip lunch that day. She had received an anonymous phone call about my eating lunch with the black students. The caller threatened that something terrible would happen to me or to our house if I continued to be so friendly with "those students." I told Mother that I could not give into that demand because the segregationists would win the battle of ideas, and that would be wrong.
>
> Glennys Oakes Johns, Class of 1958

The Lost Year, 1958-59

I left Little Rock when the schools were closed and enrolled in Norristown High School in Pennsylvania, a fully integrated school. Not only did I leave, but many hundreds of other talented people left the state never to return. So Arkansas lost a lot of talented people who could have been great contributors to the state. Arkansas lost; I did not.

Jackie Davis March, Class of 1960

In December 1958, segregationists placed a makeshift sign on the front lawn of Central High. It stated "CLOSED BY ORDER OF THE FEDERAL GOVERMENT." To Lloyd Erickson, the sign's spelling error and incorrect information seemed sadly appropriate.

The same small minds that would promote the closing of one of the finest educational institutions in the United States of America in order to avoid complying with the law put up a sign trying to shift the blame on someone else, and, in the process they misspelled a word on that sign!

Lloyd Erickson, Class of 1958

Little Rock voters were so angered by the events of the previous year and so aroused by the demagoguery of the times, they voted to have no high schools at all rather than integrate them. Self-limiting attitudes of this type are often practiced by those who do not recognize the rights of others or who feel threatened by the social involvement of people they dislike. Sometimes, the response is done for just plain devilment, providing a perverse delight to those who find the disruption of society more personally fulfilling than its advancement.

A formidable array of forces wanted to close Central High, remove the Little Rock Nine, and stop desegregation. Its foot soldiers were the impressionable students who had the encouragement and

105

backing of their pastors, parents, demagogic politicians, and other adults in the community. These groups were strongly opposed to any form of federal involvement, and they were willing to send their children to do their battle.

On the other side was a group of students who, for the first time in their lives, experienced the arbitrariness of majority rule and the social inequity and injustice of being denied the constitutional right to an education.

> It is a terrible thing suddenly not to have a school to go to. Especially when that school was one you loved so much and looked forward to graduating from with all your heart. Everyone in my family had graduated from Central High, and I loved it so much. I was totally crushed.
>
> Dorothy Hawn Larch, Class of 1959

The historical parallels of this experience for black and white students are striking. As a result of legally-sanctioned but ethically-flawed political leadership, white students could not go to school where and when they wished. Students of the lost class of 1959 were caught in the middle of political and social power plays. They were victims of a situation beyond their control.

Such a situation had been a reality black families since before statehood. Remarkably, though, few white families, who expressed their own outrage and disappointment seemed to note the similarity to the black experience.

During the 1958-59 school year, 326 of Central High's 535 seniors attended public schools in other districts or private schools in Arkansas, twenty went out of state, and sixty-four went to college early. Hall sent 132 of its 260 seniors to other Arkansas schools, sixty-three went out of state, and fifty-two went to college. About 85 percent of seniors from the all-white schools continued their educations that year. The closure took a heavier toll on the all-black Horace Mann High School, where nearly half of the seniors did not go to school at all.[76] In all, 3,261 white students and 1,069 blacks were denied education in Little Rock public schools during the "Lost Year" of 1958-59.[77]

Some students who enrolled in other districts found they had been preceded by a reputation as a Central High troublemaker.

> The principal knew I was from Little Rock, and on my first day he called me in to find out if I was going to cause trouble. I told him that if I wanted to cause trouble, I would have jumped out of one of the windows in Little Rock and then I could have had national coverage. I told him I was there for an education and that was it.
>
> Jackie Davis March, Class of 1960

Little Rock teachers had to report to the empty schools every day because of their contracts, but there was no one to teach. At Central High, a teacher recalled, they sometimes instructed each other in sewing, typing, and foreign languages. They started a faculty choir. One afternoon, they played "hide and seek" inside the vacant building.[78] Eventually, the district started using the high school teachers as substitutes in the lower grades. But for the first two months, they reported every day to their empty classrooms. Some teachers worked as tutors to groups of students in private homes. Because they were forbidden by court order to instruct students during school hours, they waited until precisely 3:30 p.m. to begin their lessons.

A series of judicial decisions (including reversals of earlier decisions) granted, and then denied, the Little Rock School District a delay for implementation of its integration plan. The most significant delay was the closing of all Little Rock high schools, and with it came the ending of school extracurricular activities, including football.

This last decision caused great anguish to Little Rock sports fans. Central High had reigned supreme in Arkansas high school football circles, winning every state championship since 1951 and all but one since 1946. The Tigers' three-year, 33-game winning streak was on the line. Even Faubus felt the pain, and he saw the School Board's decision to close football as another opportunity to shift the blame.

"Blossom and his advisors did this in a war of psychology or a cold war," Faubus told the press. He also said the denial of football was "a cruel and unnecessary blow to school children," implying that the School Board was trying to turn public sentiment against him for closing the schools. This was the first sign of growing opposition to the school closures. After the governor's prodding, the School Board rescinded the order and the Central High team missed only one practice. Other than the team and its coaches, no one seemed troubled by the absurdity of high school sports being played in a closed high school.

> We played a full football schedule without having one day of school. In fact, we had cheerleaders, the band, and pep rallies in the school auditorium with only 20 some-odd students, probably the football team, and the faculty up there doing the cheers.
>
> Clyde Hart, Head Track Coach

A new Arkansas ruling allowed Little Rock students to play football as long as they were taking correspondence courses from the University of Arkansas. If they enrolled in another school district, they became ineligible. Despite winning their first two games of the season, which increased the Central High winning streak to thirty-five games, the 1958 team lost its third game 42-0 to Istrouma High School at Baton Rouge, Louisiana. A teacher who accompanied the team on the bus ride to the game recalled that the trip included a glimpse of the dark days ahead.

> We had banners that read "Little Rock Central High Tigers" on the sides of the chartered bus. We stopped in Natchez, Mississippi, for lunch and were treated very badly. They obviously did not want to serve us because we were from that horrible school in Little Rock. We left and stopped a short distance away to remove all banners from the bus. We didn't talk about our school at any other stops.
>
> Faculty Name Withheld

108

The crushing defeat at Baton Rouge ended Central High's football dynasty and demoralized the players. By the time Hall and Central played each other on Thanksgiving Day, both squads were down to third-string players for some positions. Despite all those problems, Central's team, playing on pride and determination, finished the year second in the state with an 8-3-1 record.

Harassment of Teachers

At the end of the 1957-58 school year, I resigned my position and entered the business world in Little Rock. The events of that year changed the course of my life and career. To say the least, I had become disenchanted with my chosen profession.

Faculty Name Withheld

Early in the 1957 school year, the backlash began against educators and administrators who adhered to the rule of law and implemented school desegregation plans. On Thursday, September 5, the third day of school, petitions seeking the immediate discharge of Blossom were being circulated among the spectators gathered at Central High. The petition was not successful, but many leading figures did leave Central High or Little Rock within the next year or two. These included Superintendent Blossom, Mayor Mann, Vice Principal Powell, and others.

In addition, a rumor began to circulate that young teachers who had signed a contract to work at Central High in 1957 were members of the Communist Party. This fear mongering, which capitalized on the anti-Communist propaganda spouted by McCarthy and others, suggested that the new teachers were part of a plot to make public school integration in the South a reality.

In the spring of 1958, Faubus directed the Arkansas General Assembly's Legislative Council to use the Arkansas State Police Criminal Investigation Division to interview Central High staff. Powell was interviewed on March 6, 1958. The Little Rock School Board was concerned enough to arrange for the services of a court reporter to transcribe the discussion. In that transcript, Powell was questioned by two state police officers who told him they were seeking information that might help other Arkansas school districts learn how to have a smooth school desegregation process.

"Our main objective is for the benefit of the children," the interviewers told Powell. Their questions concerned student discipline, grades, teacher attitudes, and future plans for enrolling black students at Central High. While the transcript contains no questions on Powell's political beliefs, his responses seem very cautious and brief. He repeatedly reminded the men he had no information about student grades or other aspects of the district-wide desegregation plan.

The transcript also includes some editorial comments by Powell, who later would write, "The investigation was in many cases as plainly distasteful to the Criminal Investigation operatives as it was to everyone interviewed," and less than one fourth of the information collected "threw any educational light on our problem at Central High."

Typing teacher Carol Ann Lackey Patterson and her roommate, another Central High teacher, were also interviewed. The women, younger and less experienced in the ways of Arkansas politics than Powell, were quite apprehensive about the discussion.

> Two Arkansas state troopers showed up at the door of our apartment. They proceeded to ask us all sorts of questions. To say that my roommate and I were nervous would be an incredible understatement. We had no way of knowing what they had written in their notes or what they planned to do with the information.
>
> Carol Ann Lackey Patterson, Typing Teacher

Patterson said she often wondered if the information obtained from the teacher interviews by the State Police influenced the firing of many of the Central High faculty the following year. Both Patterson and her roommate had moved to other cities by that time, but she recalled many teacher friends who lost their jobs in what has become known as "The Purge," a May 1959 act of direct retribution against forty-four teachers and administrators by three segregationist members of a newly-elected and reconstituted school board.

Rumors of the potential firings were heard before the 1957-58 school year ended. About twenty Central High teachers met with school board attorney Wayne Upton in the summer of 1958. Upton told them that segregationists had drawn up a list of teachers they wanted purged, and that all teachers present at the meeting were on the list.[79]

Though the school year ended with high academic and athletic achievement by Central students, the state of public education in Little Rock was a disaster. Speech teacher Shirley "Micky" McGalin Dunaway said at the end of the year that teachers and students alike were equally injured and everyone felt like they were walking wounded. But their trials were not yet over.

Faubus, in the wake of his failure to prohibit the court-ordered desegregation of schools through the deployment of the Arkansas National Guard, made another bold and equally absurd move. He ordered all public high schools in the city closed. Again, the pretense was a concern for public safety. A public referendum on September 25, 1958, endorsed that decision. Little Rock residents voted 19,470 to 7,561 to close all city high schools immediately rather than integrate.

With the closing of schools, Little Rock high school teachers faced a year of confusion. Technically, they were still under contract and required to report to their buildings each day, but no classes were conducted because there were no students to teach. Teachers were not confident they would be employed through the year.

A number of hastily organized private schools sprang up in the city, including the Little Rock Private School Corporation, which operated the T. J. Raney School. The private school, which was to be segregated and tuition-free to the public, offered contracts to the Central High teachers. The private school system had the Governor's support, and he directed the Little Rock School Board to lease its building to the private initiative. Not only could Faubus reassign public school buildings to the private initiative, he also had been authorized by the pro-segregation state legislature to direct public school tax revenue to the private school system.

Within hours of the announcement of private school plan, the Eighth Circuit Court of Appeals issued an injunction blocking it. The

Supreme Court soon issued a unanimous ruling against such "evasive schemes for segregation."[80]

While these changes and reversals were taking place, Shirley Swaim Stancil recalls, a Central High staff meeting took place early in the fall of 1958 when teachers were encouraged to revoke their contracts with the Little Rock School District and accept new contracts with the Raney school. To do so, teachers would essentially abandon Central High with its admirable past but now questionable future. They would sign up with a school that could assure them employment and did not have to comply with federal desegregation orders.

> I was amazed that only sixteen teachers refused to do this. The others signed up with the private corporation and signed a document negating their contract with the Little Rock School District. Early the next morning, the faculty was served with restraining orders from a federal judge ordering us not to negate our Central contracts. Upon arrival at Central, there was quite a scramble by those who had signed contracts to retrieve them.
>
> Shirley Swaim Stancil, Guidance Counselor

The Purge of Teachers and the STOP Campaign

The confusion caused by the court led to another result desired by segregationists. In the fall of 1958, the School Board and superintendent resigned in a body, declaring the situation to be "hopeless and helpless." With the election of a new school board, rumors gained strength of a possible purge of teachers who had fallen out of favor with the administration. Faubus himself declared that he would like to see Matthews, Powell, and Huckaby, the Central High principal and vice principals, fired immediately.[81]

The Governor got his wish on May 6, 1959, when three moderate members of the six-member school board walked out of a board meeting. The moderates, who had anticipated some action against the teachers, left the meeting as advised by attorneys and as a strategy to aid the teachers in possible litigation.[82] When the three board members remaining (all segregationists) took control, they immediately fired forty-four educators, thirty from Central High and fourteen from other Little Rock public schools. The fired staff from Central High, which included the three principals, two secretaries, and twenty-five teachers, represented one fourth of the school's faculty.

Central High had been purged of staff members who, according to segregationists, were "integrationists" or "collaborators" with integrationists. These were professional educators who had put student safety first, kept Central High open and functioning, and tried hard to maintain discipline within the school. At the head of the list was Jess Matthews, a thirty-seven-year veteran in the Little Rock school system and principal at Central High for thirteen years, a man condemned for faithfully carrying out the policies of his school board and superintendent.

In a formal statement, school board president Ed I. McKinley explained the dismissals: "For a large number there was just one reason—they are integrationists or have collaborated with integrationists.... They will be hired back if they state that they support "the public policy" of racially separate schools."[83] A *Gazette* editorial commented on McKinley's "magnificent but presumably unconscious irony" when he further described the fired educators, saying, "I don't think they fit into the harmony of the school system."[84]

Faubus gained enormous statewide and national popularity for his influence in this continuing fiasco. In the fall of 1958, he was elected to a third term and was voted number 10 in a national poll for the Most Admired Men in the World. In many people's eyes, Faubus was a hero.

The concept of being a "hero," however, can also refer to people in a defeated group who would be executed first by their enemies. In that vein, the administrators and teachers who upheld the rule of law with their commitment to the education of all students, only to be summarily discharged by the segregationist school board, are surely "heroes" in the purest sense of the word.

Several reactions to the purge quickly took shape. On the campus of the University of Arkansas, former Central High students drafted and circulated a statement of solidarity and support for their fired teachers.[85]

Declaration by Former Students at Central High School Against The Purge of Our Teachers:

We, as former students of Little Rock Central High School, join in protest of what we feel to be the malicious and unjustified reprisal of our teachers:

1. Because they are directly responsible for having built over a period of years one of the top 38 high schools in America;

2. Because they have produced more than 20 national merit scholars for each of the last two years;

3. Because they have unselfishly given many years of loyal and devoted service to both the students and the community of Little Rock as teachers and as citizens;

4. Because regardless of their personal opinions during the integration controversy, to which they are entitled as Americans, they have, without qualification or exception, acted only with their students' welfare and interest as their primary concern;

5. Because these teachers have made it possible for us, as their former students to share a feeling of pride, honor, and privilege to have attended their classes;

6. Because these teachers, with whom we have personally been associated, have dedicated their lives to molding our character and developing us as future citizens of this, our free and democratic America;

We firmly pledge our support to their cause and give our unqualified endorsement to these teachers, who have exhibited unimpeachable character as teachers and as citizens of Arkansas.

The declaration was signed "With an abiding faith in our democratic principles" by approximately 1,000 former students and delivered to Matthews.

114

The purge of teachers accelerated the community response to the continuing crisis in the schools. Previously, the Little Rock Chamber of Commerce announced that its members had voted four to one to reopen the public schools on the desegregated basis. And an anonymous group known as the Women's Emergency Committee (WEC) To Open Our Schools had organized in September 1958 when the public high schools were closed and included many prominent local women.

Now, civic leaders who had been largely silent during the school crisis came to the defense of the teachers. At a PTA meeting held at Forest Park Elementary School the evening after the purge, a resolution was passed that called on patrons to circulate petitions to recall the three segregationist board members. The petition drive gained sufficient signatures, and a school board recall election was scheduled for May 25. The proposed election, it was hoped, would lead to the reinstatement and contract security of the fired teachers, many of whom had long tenure in the district. This meeting was the genesis of what would become the Stop This Outrageous Purge, or STOP Campaign. The WEC, the first organization in the city to formally denounce the firings, aided STOP efforts from the outset.[86]

Attorney William Starr Mitchell was selected as STOP's chairman, an involvement that brought threats of retribution to his family and the loss of clients to Mitchell's law practice. As STOP became organized and visible in the community, another new organization, CROSS (Committee to Retain Our Segregated Schools), sprang up in direct opposition. After three weeks of intense campaigning and publicity from both sides, stop won the school board election. The three segregationist board members were voted out and three moderates were elected in their place. The new board then rehired thirty-nine of the forty-four teachers who had been fired.

In the summer of 1959, a federal district court ruled that the Arkansas law and public vote to close schools were unconstitutional. The School Board announced that public high schools would reopen with some blacks attending Central and Hall High Schools. To outmaneuver the Governor and segregationists, the new school board opened school two weeks early that year. Protesters marched on Central High from the Capitol. The fire department opened their hoses on them. Twenty-one of the protesters were arrested.

Two weeks later, tear gas was thrown into a building where the school board was meeting. On Labor Day 1959, dynamite was used to destroy the fire chief's car, damage a commercial building owned by the mayor, and wreck part of the school administration building. Five men were arrested and sent to prison. Faubus called the violence "sickening and deplorable," but he insisted the real blame should be placed on the integration policy of the federal government.[87]

Impact on the Community

> How much did the Governor's actions cost the people
> of Arkansas? How many businesses that might have
> moved to Arkansas chose to move elsewhere? How
> many of the citizens of Little Rock have suffered
> under the unjust reputation of being a racist?
>
> Lloyd Erickson, Class of 1958

Schools reopened for the 1959-60 year, but tensions remained high. In the spring of 1960, an Air Force jet exploded in mid air over the Hillcrest area in Little Rock. The accident produced a booming wave of sound that many people, ready to think the worst, believed was the inevitable bombing of Central High upon its reopening as a desegregated high school.

It was a trying time for the once-quiet capital of a moderate Southern state. For many people, it was a period of fear and loss, confusion, and confrontation. The consequences stretched far beyond the community of Central High students and teachers and long past the two years during which most of the action occurred.

The *Arkansas Gazette* was at the time the oldest newspaper west of the Mississippi. Its pro-integration editorial policy and writings won a Pulitzer Prize for both the paper and its outspoken editor, Harry Ashmore. Ever the public citizen, *Gazette* owner J. N. Heiskell accepted the loss of subscribers and advertising as part of the price of telling the truth and upholding the law when he responded to Ashmore's question of the cost to the *Gazette* for its position.

116

"I'm an old man," he said, "and I've lived too long to let people like that take over my city."[88]

So Ashmore aggressively responded to Faubus' grandstanding statements and acts. The *Gazette*, Ashmore wrote, would show "precisely where he is taking the people of his state in the furtherance of his political ambitions, and the terrible price all of us are going to have to pay as a result."[89]

The *Arkansas Gazette* paid an immediate price for upholding its ethical position. Dramatic drops were seen in its circulation and advertising revenues after extremists sent letters to the advertising departments of many local firms threatening boycotts of any store that advertised in the newspaper. Meanwhile, the *Arkansas Democrat*, the *Gazette*'s competition, received preferential treatment at the Statehouse and the Governor's Mansion. While the *Gazette* offered daily tirades against the segregationist resistance, the *Democrat* was cautious not to offend anybody. Years later, the *Arkansas Times* summed up these contrasting positions: "It was hard to provoke the *Democrat* into more than indifferent editorial murmurs and impossible to get the *Gazette* to shut up."[90]

Over time, the *Democrat* gained and surpassed its once-incomparable rival. The paper changed to a morning delivery and began a circulation war with the *Gazette*. In 1986, the *Gazette* was sold to the Gannett chain. Within another five years, Gannett also surrendered. Little Rock's only daily newspaper became the *Arkansas Democrat-Gazette*.

The state's black newspaper, the *Arkansas State Press*, was also adversely affected. National advertisers dropped their ads. The newspaper also had been critical of black leaders it considered complacent, which caused a rapidly diminishing circulation. The newspaper was "a survivor of terror, but a victim of boycott."[91]

Apathy and Guilt

In a recurring dream that has continued now for nearly half a century, I roam the halls of Central High, aware that I am scheduled somewhere in the building for a class that goes on without me and which, in my

117

dreams I am never able to locate. It's as though I lost
something there that cannot be found again.

Larry Taylor, Class of 1959

The reflections of Central High students from 1957-58 cover a range of emotions and psychological states. These feelings can be categorized into two simple groupings: fulfilled or unsatisfied.

In the grouping of fulfilled emotions, a few students express feelings of satisfaction. They speak of what they saw and what they did with a degree of personal comfort. They are at peace with their memories of how they participated in those eventful years.

Further within this group, some students experienced a rare and wonderful breakthrough, achieving a change in the heart that forever altered how they perceived the world and how they reacted with people different from themselves.

But some students remain dissatisfied and offer a troubling personal history. To them, the new situation was threatening and challenging, involving issues not previously addressed by their culture and their upbringing. Many of these students feel they were unprepared for the situations they were placed in and the decisions they were required to make.

Fifty years later, some former students have misgivings about how they acted because of that lack of preparation and a lack of guidance at the time. Many of them use terms such as "apathy" or "indifference." They are often apologetic, and in their recollections they seek some forgiveness for things that were in their power but which they neglected to do.

Further within the unsatisfied group, many students believe they have been falsely identified over time and held up to an inaccurate public review. Some of this group believe they did everything within their power and within the opportunities offered them. Others in this same group feel they could have done more. But their overriding dissatisfaction is due to the belief they have been incorrectly judged and often pre-judged with no opportunity to explain the circumstances that actually occurred. As a group, the students wish for a more comprehensive public understanding of their actions, one that includes better awareness of the community and family issues they faced.

118

As a 17-year old in the days of strict segregation, it's difficult to imagine doing anything other than what I did, and that was to do nothing to cause trouble. My parents were certainly not integrationists, but they understood that things were changing, and like it or not they accepted it. They told me in no uncertain terms that I was to stay out of trouble and mind my own business. Today my feeling about "the year" is one of resentment toward those who paint the white students as a bunch of enablers who stood back and watched as rabid segregationists brutalized the Nine.

Lee "Andy" Johnson, Class 1958

This student, who followed his parents' advice and minded his own business, was not apathetic. Key definitions of the term "apathy" include indifference, boredom, and lack of interest in the events. The student expressed none of these. Nor did he express remorse. The student made a deliberate choice to follow the rule of law and his parents' wishes. The majority of the white students at Central High made a similar choice.

This student and the group he represents were not enablers. To label them as such is to blur the distinction between not caring and not having an opportunity to act. It is equally wrong to fault this group for not demonstrating heroic behavior. Most students had neither the opportunity nor the temperament to be heroes. They simply conducted themselves with restraint and composure in an extremely challenging time. That behavior may not merit the highest praise, but it certainly does not justify a condemnation.

Several students do use the word "apathy," but for the most part they are actually describing regret for a personal act of withholding friendship or compassion.

Carlotta Walls was the only black student I ever got into contact with and the first black person I had ever known by name. I didn't make an effort to befriend her. I observed from a distance and never even said "Hello." I am sorry about my apathetic behavior. She was a good student and she carried herself with grace, poise, and courage.

Carol MaGouirk Sanders, Class of 1960

Two junior class members of the 1957 Central High football team expressed similar sentiments of residual guilt in a 2007 *Sports Illustrated* article.

Backup running back Josh McHughs still wishes he could utter the words he wanted to but didn't: "It's going to be all right, Elizabeth..." Starting running back Ronnie Spann wishes he introduced himself to Carlotta Walls in biology class instead of keeping his distance. "But the coach and my parents kept saying, 'Stay out of it,' and the kids who were friendly to blacks got ostracized, and I was a kid just trying to fit in. If I saw her now, I'd say I'm sorry I didn't hug you and hold your hand. If I could do it over, I'd be a friend."[92]

If anyone should have been a hero, it would have been a football player on the best high school team in the nation. We tend to romanticize these characters as larger-than-life figures, young men with great capacity for leadership. And in truth, a few of them had those qualities.

But the larger truth is that all of them were 17 or 18 year-old adolescents with teenage fears and aspirations. Given the training and opportunity to act, they certainly could have interceded physically in a racial encounter if one occurred in their presence. But the football team members, far more than other students, were directed by a coach they highly respected to avoid all encounters Violation of that rule would mean immediate dismissal from the team. To hold them liable for not seeking out situations in which to intercede is unfair and unreasonable.

Additionally, students should not be held liable for actions and influence outside their scope of assigned responsibility. Their task was not to seek out and correct problem students. That job belonged to

Little Rock's School Superintendent, and Central High's principal and vice principals, who, despite knowing the problem students' identities, were unable to fully control them. Some troublemakers probably received praise from their parents and community for their disruptive actions at school.

Nor can Central High students be expected to have responded to rumors, which is all most of them had. Full knowledge of the incidents and the perpetrators was denied to all students and athletes by the confidential nature of the school's disciplinary procedures. No student disciplinary panel had ever been used before, and none was empanelled that year. Further, when persistent rumors or newspaper reports prompted student leaders to offer their help, school administrators politely turned them down with the response that "Everything is under control."

Finally, holding students responsible for not intervening when acts of harassment occurred in their presence overlooks the discouragement of that intervention. An incident described in *Crisis at Central High* offers an interesting example. Due to death threats because of her father's position, which started on Thursday night August 30, Gail Blossom, the superintendent's daughter, stayed out of school for the first week. On Tuesday September 11, when she came to school for the first time, football player Bruce Fullerton was asked by Principal Matthews to watch over Gail in the school hallways that day. In her book, Huckaby wrote that she observed Fullerton following behind Gail to assure her safety for the next few days.[93]

This situation of one student's assuming personal responsibility for another was based on the shared history and established friendship of these two persons. The same assurance of personal safety cannot realistically be expected from the overall student body toward the nine new black students. White students had no shared history with the blacks, no introduction to them as individuals (as the welcome program might have provided), and no encouragement from school administrators to interact in any way more than a courteous manner.

At Central High, every student had total responsibility for his or her own individual conduct, but little or no responsibility for the conduct of others. And the observant problem students quickly realized and capitalized on that.

Changes in the Heart

My class was the end of an era of innocence.

Roberta Martin Moore, Class of 1958

I changed to someone who felt a real sense of compassion for these students, and felt like they deserved something that I had. I think at that point is when I really began to change my mind and realize that this was not a states' rights issue, it was a people issue.

Craig Rains, Class of 1958,
quoted in the PBS Series, "Eyes on the Prize"

Systemic social change occurs more as evolution than revolution. Passing years and generations are required for the dramatic events, the harbingers of change, to be assimilated into the minds of a people and become part of their lives and culture. Many Central High students experienced those dramatic moments. They frequently took place in the crowds at school or on city streets, in passing brief interactions, oftentimes encompassing only the smallest gestures, the unintentional connections. Yet they overflowed with deep and lasting meaning.

These are the changes in the heart. All Central High students, white and black, were changed by these experiences and the dramatic realizations that accompanied their new understanding. Some years before she attended Central High, Yvonne Thompson had such an experience.

My first consciousness of racial differences came in the summer of 1953—I was 13. One summer afternoon, I caught the bus home from the library. I was very tanned from hours riding horseback in the sun. A few minutes after I boarded the bus, the driver stopped in the middle of a block, not a regular stop, got out of his seat, approached me, and ordered me to leave my seat and move to the back of the bus. I was at first confused, then shocked and angry. I realized he thought I was a "Nigra." I had noticed they usually sat at the back of the bus, but I didn't think much about it or know why. I told him, "No." He became agitated and told me I would either move to the back or he would throw me off the bus. I told him I would sit where I wanted. He told me to get off the bus. He was big, menacing, and angry. I had been taught to respect authority, although at that moment I began to question all of that. I got off and walked home furious. Without realizing it or understanding anything about the issue, I had just been introduced to the world of segregation and Jim Crow laws.

Yvonne Thompson, Class of 1958

For Carolyn Glover Hirby, a personal understanding of what it meant to be a black person came as a result of a chance street encounter. Waiting at a bus stop in front of a donut shop in downtown Little Rock, Hirby was approached by an elderly black woman, her family's maid, with a few coins in her hand. The woman asked Hirby to use the money to purchase a donut for her. Entering the shop with the money, Hirby was shocked when the owner told her he would accept the money, but the black woman could not come inside and choose her own donut.

Over the years, I have remembered that day, her face, his attitude, and my embarrassment. When you stand there with a donut in your hand that you purchased for a lady that could not walk into the shop simply because she was black, discrimination becomes a reality that must be reckoned with.

Carolyn Glover Hirby, Class of 1960.

123

Two Central High female students shared recollections of small, intimate encounters with their black classmates. The connections were momentary, but they left lasting impressions.

I had a biology class with Minnijean Brown. I remember seeing her get up and run out of class with tears in her eyes. In the restroom, Minnijean was crying her eyes out. I put my arm around her and asked her what the matter was. She said someone in class she thought was her friend had called her a n**** and made some other uncalled for remarks. She was so hurt. Imagine having very few friends in school, then finding out that one of them had just turned on you.

Mary Ann Rath Marion, Class of 1959

After lunch, girls would gather in the restroom to put on fresh lipstick and to brush their hair. In those days, girls wore white blouses and full skirts, with lots of petticoats. We would flip our skirts up and pull the shirttail of our blouses down smoothly. Then we would straighten our skirts and were off for the next class. One day, Elizabeth Eckford was in the restroom. She was standing alone, at the back of the crowd. No one spoke to her. As I flipped my skirt up, she flipped her skirt up. Our eyes met and we smiled. I began to think about how Elizabeth had feelings, just as I did. I couldn't get her out of my mind for the rest of the day.

Nancy Brandt, Class of 1960

Most of the emotional student recollections, the stories that most profoundly reveal the workings of the heart, are from females. Male students surely had similar encounters, but very few brought forth those personal and human connections in their histories. More characteristic of the male response was a comment from football team member Bill May, who said his Central High experience occurred when he began learning about race in America. "If I was black, I'd have ended up a Black Panther," May said.[94]

Other than the Little Rock Nine, who are the heroes of Central High? The teachers and administrators who were fired by the segregationist school board in the May 1959 purge would deny being heroes. They would describe themselves as only the more visible members of the Central High faculty and staff who deserve equal credit for bringing the school through that year successfully. The observations of Betty Jane "B. J." Leggett Chick may offer the closer answer:

> The witnessing of hatred toward the nine black students was a significant turning point for me. I had not, before that time, seen openly expressed hatred. My conceptual framework of the world had suddenly been changed and the world was no longer safe and good. It became clear that now was the time to take an unpopular stand and speak out about my convictions and beliefs. I made it my mission to support the nine students that year in any way that I could. I would offer a smile, greet them in the hallways and in class, and let my opinions be known.

Chick's deliberate efforts were soon curtailed by her father, who explained how her friendliness to the black students had brought phone calls and bombs threats to his business. "I distinctly remember his words to me," she said. "Be very careful. Remember that what you say and do can seriously affect the business, and don't get involved!"

Chick was highly visible among students because of her senior year position as captain of the Central High "High Steppers," a precision marching group that performed at athletic events. In response to her father's request that she restrain her public gestures to the black students, Chick began making phone calls to express her respect and support. The calls were difficult because of her shyness. She remembers her calls to Ernest Green were timed specifically on Sunday nights after he had returned home from church.

Chick said Green was quiet and soft-spoken, and her comments were often followed by a long quiet pause and a brief "Thank you." Chick said she would to try to engage Green in a conversation, asking him about his classes and his church that night. His replies were brief and not open-ended for further exchange. Although the calls were not smooth interactions, Chick said she felt she had done something to express her support of the black students' presence that year.

But her personal involvement could not protect her from the ultimate realization of the world in which she lived. For the heroes of Central High, black and white, there were no happy endings.

> I recall the disbelief and heartache I felt the night after a boy spit on Minnijean outside of home economics class. I also recall graduation night. Ernest was called to the stage to receive his diploma and there were resounding BOOs from the audience. I was shocked and in disbelief that after the full school term, the hatred still existed. My world would never be the same.
>
> Betty Jane "B. J." Leggett Chick, Class of 1958

Voices From Central High: The Mob Outside

I had never seen a riot or given any thought to what one would be like until before my very eyes one was rapidly unfolding as I stood in the window of the second story study hall at Central High on a sultry overcast morning in early September.

Thousands of strange men and women cursing, pushing and shoving, threatening and describing what they planned for our nine new students and the Little Rock police, as well, if the police did not cease manning those white barricades and come over to their side as they expected all good white patriots should do. The yelling was fearsome, the danger was apparent and what had begun as an uncertain school day was turning into a daylight nightmare that even a kid like me knew reeked with real destructive violence.

Wendell Ross, Class of 1959

Even though I grew up in the same neighborhood where Central is located and knew many of the local residents, I never saw a single adult person in those crowds of adult hecklers and noise makers at the school that I recognized. I never saw any of my fellow students' parents in those crowds. I am still firmly convinced the noisy crowds in front of the school each morning were made up of "outsiders" who came to Little Rock to be sure not to miss anything that might happen during the initial phase of integration.

Ralph Brink, Sr., Class of 1958

I have fairly vivid memories of the first day the "Little Rock Nine" attempted to enter Central. Some students walked out and joined the crowd of onlookers outside. I stayed in class, but I heard chants outside; two in particular stick with me: "Two, four, six, eight, We ain't gonna integrate" and "Two, four, six, eight, ten, We ain't gonna let the n**** in."

Paul Redditt, Class of 1960

Football Coach Wilson Matthews, after observing the melee outside, said, "It looks like blacks outside were being killed." Tackle Bubba Crist saw whites smash the car window of two black construction workers with a shovel and drag the men out and beat them.

"Blindsided by History," Sports Illustrated

Chapter 4

Personal Motivation

Student Values

My senior year at Central High, I was in a carpool of people who had varying views toward the integration issue. One was a rabid segregationist and offered his views constantly which eventually turned all of us against him. I wanted my education and I saw nothing religiously, economically, or socially wrong with going to school with a Negro.

Beach Carre, Class of 1958

The day the nine black students gained entrance to the school, a cousin came to my classroom to get me to walk out with him, and I remember refusing to do so. I didn't do this out of any great sense of morality or human rights, but mostly because of that excitement at being at the epicenter of something big. Years later I ran into the teacher of that geometry class, Mrs. Reiman, and she told me she had witnessed my refusal to leave and had always remembered it with great pride as an example of doing the right thing. I wish I had deserved it a little more.

Charles E. "Chuck" Bell, Class of 1960

I was relieved when the 101st Airborne came because we had some political support to guarantee that order and discipline were to be maintained both inside and outside Central. For once we weren't alone in meeting these responsibilities. By this time, all the seniors wanted was for someone to guarantee that we would finish our senior year.

Ralph Brodie, Class of 1958

When Craig Rains was interviewed in 1997 at the fortieth anniversary of Central High's desegregation, he spoke of a change of heart he had experienced forty years earlier.[96] In a September 5, 1957 interview with the *Arkansas Gazette*, the teenaged Rains disapproved of integration and predicted violence at his school. "I think Faubus did right in using the National Guard," he said at the time.

In the morning before that interview, Rains was performing his school duties, raising the American flag on the school's front lawn. In a moment of startling drama, he saw Elizabeth Eckford being turned away from the school by the Guard and followed by adults and teenagers screaming insults at her. He walked beside her in the street for a short distance while he recorded the event with his camera. Perhaps the words of the Pledge of Allegiance, "with liberty and justice for all," were still echoing in his mind when on September 23, he stood again at the flagpole and witnessed a group of white thugs kick and punch a black reporter.

Rains said the two scenes troubled him deeply and led to a new philosophy.

If those kids wanted to come to my school and get an education, then I was all for it. I don't think my original opposition had anything to do with the students being black, but just that we were doing something we were being forced to do. I probably would have been against it, too, if we had been forced to accept white students from North Little Rock.

Craig Rains, Class of 1958

The mob violence outside of Central High troubled many students. Those disruptions were subtly acknowledged in an award-winning essay titled "My Pride in My American Heritage," written by Student Body Vice President Janice Shepherd Swint.[97]

> The indifference of present day Americans toward freedom is in sharp contrast to the attitude of Americans two centuries ago. The world prestige and liberties, which we enjoy today, were handed down to us by men and women who were willing to fight and die for them.... In America a man's life is what he makes it, for it is not determined by any social caste...An American citizen is also offered an excellent educational program. This program is extended to all through the free public school system. The door to higher education stands open to anyone who desires to enter.
>
> Janice Shepherd Swint, Class of 1958

Student experiences at Central High reinforced many of the values instilled in those young people by their families and their churches. The building itself also positively influenced students with its stylized grandeur, its broad halls with tiled floors, and its high ceilings.

> I loved that big beautiful building called Central High, the long hallways, the rows and rows of lockers, the cafeteria, and most of all, the auditorium. There was just something about being in there that held a special magic for me.
>
> Sherrie Smith Oldham, Class of 1958

Built in 1927 at a cost of $1.5 million and designed for up to 3,000 students, Little Rock High School was hailed as the most expensive, most beautiful, and largest high school in the nation.[98] Its opening earned national publicity with nearly 20,000 people attending the dedication ceremony.[99] The school's name was changed to Little Rock

131

Central High School in 1955, two years after plans for a second high school were announced in 1953. For thirty years, Central High was the city's only white public high school, attended by the parents, grandparents, and extended families of the 1957 students.

Today, developmental psychologists speak of children rising to the expectation levels of the adults in their lives. At Central High, the expectations for excellence and a tradition of achievement were an essential part of the school's identity and history. Certainly, the middle group of Central High students was composed of average students and achievers. However, a small number of students likely descended to the low expectations of their adult community and negatively acted out as they were encouraged to do.

But a pervasive expectation for excellence characterized Central High's academic, athletic, and citizenship activities. The Class of 1958 had a group of top achievers who felt a competitive push to surpass previous school achievements.

> Our school's 30-year history since 1927 was full of achievements against which we were going to be measured. Being runner-up, just a contender or challenger, was never an acceptable choice. Being challenged to be more, to be better, to excel, to win, to be number one was what Central High was all about. The real challenge, however, was not only to excel but to be well-rounded and make your grades as well. It was what our parents, teachers, coaches, and the community expected.
>
> Ralph Brodie, Class of 1958

Students who felt the push to excel could choose among many academic courses and extracurricular activities at the large school. Debate, cheerleading, band, spirit squad, football, basketball, and track offered broad opportunities. In their two previous years at Central High, the senior class of 1958 had gained the confidence to surpass the school's already high achievements. That preparation also gave some of them a keen insight into the inequities of the world in which they lived.

132

I knew from my conversations with Ernest Green that his preparation for our physics class and our college prep courses was not as good as what I had received at Central High. It was clear to me that "separate but equal" was absolutely not true.

Glennys Oakes Johns, Class of 1958

Academics and Citizenship

I remember Mrs. Reiman being very adamant about Student Council representatives conducting themselves in the highest way. Some students tried to protest in a silent way by wearing black on a predetermined day, but Mrs. Reiman was very concerned that no Student Council Representative was participating in this demonstration because we were supposed to set an example and be leaders.

Jenny Lee Shumate, Class of 1960

All students have stories about a favorite teacher who exposed them to the issues and values of the larger world, a person who helped cultivate the students' capacity to understand and interact on new levels.

A. L. Lape, my band director, absolutely refused to let members of his band get caught up in all of the disruption taking place around us, even though we could look out of our fifth floor homeroom every morning and, after the arrival of the 101st Airborne, see the gun placements on the roof of our school. Or Josephine Feiock, my English teacher, who was convinced that her students were going to graduate from high school with the ability to both speak and write the King's English, or we would have to deal with her. Without teachers like these, who did their utmost to ignore the socio-political events swirling around them—as well as other members of our faculty whose only concerns were educating their students, to the best of their ability, it is difficult to imagine what could have happened to the education process that year.

Woody Mann, Class of 1958

The graduating class of 1957 had twenty-two National Merit Semifinalists, earning the school an academic ranking among the Top 38 high schools in the nation. The 1958 graduating class, despite the enormous disruptions of that school year, included nineteen National Merit Semifinalists, 13 percent of all those selected in Arkansas.

Another seven National Merit Semifinalists can be credited to Central High in 1958. These were students who transferred to the new Hall High School for their senior years.[100] Those students had been taught by Central High's teachers as sophomores and juniors. Because the National Merit Exam is usually taken during the first two months of the school year, the combined total of twenty-six National Merit Semifinalists for Central and Hall High in 1957-58 was due to the academic influence of Central High.

Achievements of this magnitude reflect the outstanding work of a committed faculty. Many Central High students from that time have strong recollections of the educators who influenced them.

My eleventh-grade American History teacher, Miss Emily Penton, left a great impression. She demanded nothing but respect. And she got it! She never used the blackboard. She never had a written test paper. She never used an overhead or a movie film. She would just tell you the story of America. She could stare at you, and you crawled into the corner if you didn't focus. She had a magic that I have never seen before or since.

John Taylor, Class of 1959

When the high schools closed in 1958-59, the Little Rock School District began offering televised classes, and Penton was selected to give the eleventh-grade American History class. That process was soon prohibited by the courts, but Penton's historical commentary on how America came to be had already gained a large audience. According to Taylor, so many viewers contacted the television station that a six a.m. television show, "Good Morning with Miss Emily," was scheduled. Penton told stories from American history for the remainder of the school year.

Teachers like Penton and the variety and quality of programs at Central High were superior to many offered in surrounding school districts. As a result, white parents in those communities often made tuition arrangements or accommodations with relatives and friends at Little Rock to have their children enrolled at Central High.

Teacher dedication did not waiver during the 1957 crisis. The faculty had been instructed by Matthews to maintain discipline and to teach. They did so by consistently maintaining an atmosphere of normalcy. The political problem was the Governor's responsibility. The education of students was theirs, and they were determined that no one, not even the governor, was going to stop them from continuing what they had been doing for many years.

Mr. Matthews and the two Vice Principals, Mrs. Elizabeth Huckaby and Mr. J. O. Powell, were each like The Rock of Gibraltar through all the upheaval and unrest. They received threatening phone calls, verbal and written abuse, but they were always in control, which was very reassuring to the teachers. The faculty members became a close group that nurtured each other as sometimes happens when individuals are placed in situations of danger or great stress.

Carol Ann Lackey Patterson, Typing Teacher

Many Central High teachers believe they were able to meet their professional responsibilities because of Matthews' leadership. He wanted the desegregation process to succeed and the school year to

135

continue as normally as possible. He wanted his teachers to be able to teach, his students to grow, the school to maintain its excellent national reputation. In normal times, his positive influence on the Central High staff would have been exemplary. For his work and suffering in that turbulent year of desegregation, Industrial Arts teacher Paul Magro said, Matthews should have received the Freedom Medal.

> When we spoke with Matthews, his response was to maintain our dignity, protect our students, and teach as though it was a normal time. He was criticized by some for not expelling all of the troublemakers. We must remember, five decades later, that school discipline and policy is not the same. Back then, study hall and on-site discipline were generally effective. An expulsion was very final and, often, the expelled student did not finish school. As an educator, this was not Matthews' goal for a student.
>
> Elizabeth Riggs Brandon, English Teacher

Citizenship Training at Boys State and Girls State

Since 1940, the American Legion in Arkansas has sponsored Arkansas Boys State, a one-week summer program for high school juniors. A corresponding program, Arkansas Girls State, has functioned since 1942. The programs include lectures on democratic ideals and philosophies, stories of famous American leaders, and participation in elections for offices in mock cities, counties, and states. The programs had a distinct influence on the citizenship and respect for the law exhibited by Central High student leaders. In turn, these students had a strong influence on their classmates through their high visibility as both athletes and school leaders.

Central High sent seventy-one members of its junior class to Boys and Girls State in 1957. Some of the delegates transferred to Hall High School that fall, but approximately eight to ten percent of Central High's 603 graduating seniors in 1958 attended the summer programs as juniors.

The programs have been a training ground for future politicians and civic leaders. That influence on young people gained national exposure through a brief film clip widely used in the 1992 presidential elections. The film showed a young Bill Clinton as a Boys State delegate to Boys Nation in 1963 shaking hands with his idol, President John F. Kennedy, on the White House lawn.

Elections of Central High students to officer positions at Girls and Boys State in the summer of 1957 reflected the quality of students attending and the high esteem in which they were held by their peers. Three Central High girls—Janice Shepherd, Gail Blossom and Madge Gregory—were elected as associate justices of the Girls State Supreme Court, Justlyn Matlock was elected to the Legislature, and Helen Ruth Smith was runner-up in the Lieutenant Governor's election.

Central High boys made history earlier that summer when Ralph Brodie and Bill Hicks were elected Boys State Governor and Lieutenant Governor, respectively. It was the first time that Boys State's top two officers had been selected from the same school. Two additional Central High students were elected to top positions: Ronnie Hubbard as Treasurer, and Bruce Fullerton as Senator and Boys Nation delegate.

In the summer of 1958, a Central High student again made history at Boys State when, for the first time, a school's delegate was elected governor two years in a row. Wendell Ross was elected Boys State Governor, and Central High students won an additional four top positions that summer.

"The over-arching theme of the American Legion program was the rule of law," Brodie said. "We were taught respect for the courts and saw the fundamental basis of our democracy at work in the privilege of voting."

Brodie did not remember any racist comments or overt actions in the summer of 1957. Although he did learn some years later that a number of the Legionnaires who were responsible for Boys State in 1957 held strong segregationist attitudes, their views were not evident at the time, he added.

With training in the "rule of law" so recently impressed on them, the Central High delegates to Boys State and Girls State returned to school in the fall of 1957 and watched in dismay as the high ideals of democracy and equal opportunity were trampled on by state politicians and community leaders. The students were better prepared than most, however, to resist those forces with that training behind them.

The lessons of respect for the law were again challenged in 1958 when Brodie, as Boys State Governor, presided over the summer sessions and introduced the invited guest speakers and elected officials who addressed the delegates.

"When Governor Faubus came and I realized I had to introduce him, I had to fight the pain and disgust I had for the man who brought shame and dishonor to Central High, Little Rock, and Arkansas," Brodie said. "Nonetheless, I tried to, and I think did, introduce him with the respect and courtesy his office deserved. Little did I know the worst was yet to come."

After Faubus' introduction at Girls State in the summer of 1958, several of us from Little Rock Central refused to stand as he walked on stage to speak to the delegates. Our counselors made us stand to show our respect for the office, if not for him. I stood about half way up and would not applaud.

Mary Ann Rath Marion, Class of 1959

Parents and Community

I recall lying in bed through September nights, the windows open, hearing the wails of sirens. My father would say, "There is a lot of meanness going on in this city tonight."

One morning I gave a ride to my Latin teacher, Mrs. Abby Foster, to her home to retrieve a book. On the way, she asked me of my plans. I told her I planned to be a minister. There was a brief silence as my car rolled forward. Then Mrs. Foster replied, "That's good. Preach a little love. Preach a little love."[101]

Larry Taylor, Class of 1959

Teachers, as surrogate parents for some young people, can be as influential for role modeling and citizenship as the training provided in a home. But the home environment, through everyday dinner conversations and the real-life experiences parents share with their children, has a unique opportunity to instill deep values of tolerance and ethical guidance. Roberta Martin Moore, Class of 1958, recalled school-based training in patriotism and an accompanying morality. But she said ethics did not have to be taught because "most of us learned that from our parents."

In 1954, as our family sat down to dinner, my parents explained the decision just rendered by the Supreme Court in <u>Brown vs. Board of Education</u>. They said everyone was entitled to a good education, that black children could not be denied entrance into white schools based on race... and that this was the law of the land. We had a lively family discussion about the decision. We, as a family, would abide by this law.

Ann Williams Wedaman, Class of 1959

In my family, I was raised to treat all people with equal respect. The "N" word was not used, ever. Our family employed a black cleaning lady, who actually half raised me, and I could never understand why she would not sit down and eat lunch with me. But, again, I was raised to be respectful to her as my elder and do what she said to do, and also to be kind to all people and always to be thinking of how my words and actions would affect them.

Dorothy Hawn Larch, Class of 1959

Rather than participate in acts of angry rebellion or defiance toward integration, my parents chose to be an example before me. I never left for school, without my

139

fears, my choices, and my safety being prayed over by my loving parents. I am grateful for their support and wise counsel in keeping my head and my heart focused on the right path in my formative years.

Carolyn Glover Hirby, Class of 1960

Two Central High senior students in 1957, Woody Mann, the mayor's son, and Ralph Brodie, student body president, have credited family influences to strongly shaping the students' values and providing them with the ethical guidance to successfully negotiate the challenges of their final year of high school.

One of the most visible and active participants in the Central High situation, Mayor Mann had never been a supporter of classroom integration. Rather, he saw himself as a practical and honest civil servant, committed to upholding the law of the land, who was forced to take a stand against the governor's racist agitation. "Mann did what needed to be done and stood up," said Roy Reed, Faubus' biographer, "and it cost him whatever future he had in politics in Arkansas."[102]

Mann and his family received death threats, and crosses were burned on his front lawn. His son Woody had a police security escort during the Central High crisis period. When his term as mayor ended in 1958, Mann moved to Dallas, where he returned to the insurance business. Mann died in 2002 at the age of 85.

When my Dad was elected a mayor of Little Rock in 1955, I really didn't think it was any big deal. Several of my friends thought it was pretty cool to run around with the "Mayor's kid," but to me life seemed pretty much the same after he was elected mayor as it had been before.

As a young man, he enrolled in the Navy, and he served for a time in the Pacific on the staff of Admiral Chester Nimitz. After the service, he returned to his beloved Little Rock to open his own insurance agency.

My dad always loved people—he never met a stranger, and one of his favorite admonitions to me was "Son, when you walk down the hall at school, look people in the eye and say 'Hello.'" That, along with a "firm handshake" and "stand up straight and keep your shoulders back," were always directions to me from him.

From the time he took office in January 1956, his tenure as mayor seemed to be marked by controversy. Never much for maintaining the status quo, he made significant changes in the way City Hall was run, which did not sit well with several alderman on the City Council. He was not part of the "Good Ole Boy" system which, at the time, was the way that Little Rock's political system functioned.

One of my favorites of his sayings is "All it takes for evil to prevail is for good men to stand idly by and do nothing." My dad did not adhere to that philosophy. He entered the arena and got his nose bloodied, but he taught me that if you risk nothing, you lose nothing. If you never play the game, you never know the joy of victory or the taste of defeat, all of which shape and mold a person's character.

Although far from perfect, he was my dad, and I loved him for who and what he was. I was proud of him for what he did—at great personal sacrifice. I think he always knew that. He was my dad—he was my hero.

Woody Mann, Class of 1958

Brodie was probably the white student with the highest profile at Central High during the crisis. Brodie was written up in the *Arkansas Democrat* as his graduation date drew near. The article described him as one who "commands respect because the quietness with which he surrounds himself is the calm of a person at peace with himself."[103]

141

After his ambush interview with Mike Wallace on the first day of school, Brodie did not talk to reporters, claiming he could not be a spokesman for the majority of the students. He said he did not know how the majority felt. Journalists aggressively pursued him until they were threatened with restraining orders by Prosecuting Attorney Frank Holt. Brodie also refused to have his picture taken during his senior year other than as a member of Central High athletic teams. He continued to refuse interviews for the next twenty years.

The Essence of Good Citizenship

I was fortunate to have two well-educated parents, Hazel Gray and Frank T. Brodie, the first in their families to graduate from college. They believed in commitment, hard work, and most of all, personal responsibility and integrity. They were supportive of all I tried to do.

In 1954, school discipline was strict, and good conduct, manners, and high grades were expected. With rare exception, teachers and coaches were disciplinarians and had absolute control of the classrooms and the athletic teams. Principals supported the teachers 100 percent and laid down the law. In those days, parents would invariably back them up. It was an orderly, safe, and challenging time.

In junior high athletics, we were expected to learn and play by the rules. Coaches verbally chastened us if we broke any rules and removed us from play if the problems continued. At Central High, most students and I saw desegregation as just one more rule change to which we were expected to adapt. School was to go on as usual without interruption.

I wasn't overtly conscious of it growing up, but I was being molded into an individual with an appreciation of and reverence for citizenship. My parents' lives were continuing examples of these fundamental values. Being thought of as a good citizen was to bring honor not only on oneself, but also to one's family, friends, and school.

My grandfather, John Cleveland Gray, small town grocer and mayor of Monette, in northeast Arkansas, set the tone. I heard stories from my uncle that Granddad had fed half of Craighead County during the Depression and at one time carried an Accounts Due of over $250,000.

I saw Mom care for Granddad and Grandmother during the last years of their lives. She had periodically done so since she was a teenager, when Grandmother's attacks of asthma began and Granddad's periodic moroseness first started. She also raised my twin sisters, who are seven years younger than I am. She taught me love of family and duty and responsibility.

Dad lost his father and two sisters in the 1918-19 flu epidemic when he was just five years old. He served in the Navy during WWII and Korea, and he shared with me his code of conduct, honor, and citizenship. Dad was demanding in his sense of right, wrong, truth, integrity, and loyalty to friends. He insisted I always finish what I started, and he taught me personal responsibility for my own conduct and for my own advancement.

I did not realize at the time the blessings and privilege I had through my parents or how important to my life their example would be. My home and family seemed completely normal, a situation experienced by nearly all my friends and teammates

143

who also had responsible, caring parents who expected the best from them, too. That was the life in which we grew up.

Ralph Brodie, Class of 1958

Athletic Victories And Legendary Success

In southwest Little Rock, it was common on weekends for a group of white and black kids about my age to play basketball, softball, and other sports. This was my introduction to integration long before my senior year at Central, playing sports with kids of a different race. The experience helped to establish values to judge people by their abilities and not the color of their skin.

Art Pearrow, Class of 1958

The more games the football team won, the more control we seemed to have inside Central. Our undefeated season gave the student body a positive boost and helped keep morale high inside the school. That was the first indication that the year could be normal despite the outside distractions.

Ralph Brodie, Class of 1958

In neighborhood parks or on the ball fields of professional teams, athletics have introduced a social balance unacceptable in other facets of life. Children, in particular, find through games a means of overcoming the artificial barriers their parents have established between people. In the late 1950s, the introduction of supremely talented black athletes such as Willie Mays, Bill Russell, and Jim Brown demonstrated that professional sports could no longer deny the participation of black athletes.

Central High in 1957 was years away from having racially-mixed athletic teams. Nevertheless, the school's coaches produced some of the most accomplished teams in American high school sports history. Top athletes on the 1956 football team included Bill Hicks, an All-Southern selection, and Bruce Fullerton, an All-State selection. In the 1957 football season, Hicks and Fullerton were All American football players on Central's national championship team, and Fullerton was selected National Football Player of Year by *The Sporting News*. Fullerton scored twenty-seven touchdowns that season, as troops from the 101st Airborne watched and cheered each Central High home game from the 10,000-seat Quigley Field they had nicknamed "Fort Central." In addition, the 1957 team included nine athletes named All-State and twelve players who became college starters.

Ralph Brodie was a first-team player on both the 1956 and 1957 football squads, and he and Hicks also lettered on the 1957 Big 8 Championship basketball team. They were also first-string players on the state champion runner-up 1958 basketball team. On the track team, Brodie and Fullerton were part of relay teams that broke every state relay record in 1956-58. Brodie also held the state low hurdles record in 1957 and set the high hurdles record in 1958.

Star athletes, particularly the football players, were recognized on and off the field for their accomplishments. An *Arkansas Gazette* editorial credited Fullerton, Hicks, and Brodie for never having been "among the small company of Central High School students who have resorted to disorder and violence."[104] "It is not football training alone, but family background that has kept these and other members of the Tiger athletic teams out of the mob of trouble makers," the *Gazette* editor wrote. "We should be less critical in the future of competitive athletics as a training ground for citizenship."

Athletic achievement as a foundation for good citizenship had been noted a year earlier in a *Tiger* article by Principal Matthews. Matthews' article "Athletics Are Helpful to Individual, School" affirmed that "athletics inculcate in the mind courage, will power, determination and grit that are strong factors in our every day life. They build up a code of morals to be adhered to under all circumstances, whether we win or lose."[105]

Central High is one of the few American high schools to win over 100 state championships in team sports. Its legendary success includes more state titles in team sports than any other high school in the continental United States. Prior to 1957, the track team and Coach Earl Quigley had been featured in "Ripley's Believe It or Not" on three occasions: they were victorious in fifty consecutive meets; they competed for fifteen years without a defeat; and they won ninety-seven consecutive meets including eighteen consecutive state championships.[106]

The school's football team had been so successful for so long, so far above the level of any other Arkansas team, its regular season schedule had been expanded to include games with the best teams from Kentucky, Louisiana, Texas, Tennessee, and other Southern states. In the 1957 season, the team extended its three-year winning streak to thirty-three games and won its twenty-second state championship, a national record at the time.

Despite the life-changing events and attention focused on the school that year, the team was named number one in the nation by National Sports News Service of Minnesota. And in 2000, the 1957 team was listed as one of the two best high school football teams in the 1950s and among the Twelve Best High School Football Teams in the United States in the Past 100 Years.[107]

The coaches in 1957 kept their players focused on their sport rather than on what was happening on the school's lawn and in the halls. The process strengthened the students' resolve for self-discipline and staying focused on goals. Athletics, as Principal Matthews had written in *The Tiger*, contributed to the morals of the athletes.

Wilson Matthews: Head Football Coach

The most visible and vocal member of the Central High athletic staff was Football Coach Wilson Matthews (no relation to Principal Jess Matthews), whose eleven seasons at the school yielded a record of 111 wins, fourteen losses, and three ties. A Marine Corps veteran, the career coach was known for his brusque language and intimidating, hard-bitten demeanor. The *Arkansas Democrat-Gazette*, in a memorial article at the time of his death, described Matthews as:

A flesh and blood myth, a living, fire-breathing legend, as real as the stereotypes in all those black-and-white sports movies are fiction. The guy could have been an icon for ESPN classic: ball cap, farmer's tan, sweat pants bunched at the knee, whistle around the neck, white socks and black coaches' shoes, a stare that could pierce concrete.

"He was so tough on you, you could have killed him. But as you mature in life and you look back on the situation," said Eddie Bradford, who played for Matthews at Little Rock High in the 1950s, "you say that this was the making of the man. How grateful you are to be exposed to someone who had such expectations."[108]

In his last year at Central High, Matthews ran his practices around the tents, trucks, and soldiers of the 101st Airborne Division. The troops showed up at the football stadium the night they arrived in Little Rock. All the coaching staff except Wilson Matthews were there, preparing for the next game. An officer came to the coaches' area to inform them that General Walker had selected Matthews' office for his headquarters. Reached by phone with the news, Matthews reportedly said "Tell the son-of-bitch to get out."

Though he lost his office for the duration of the encampment, Matthews was not about to surrender his practice field to the troops who had set up a helicopter landing pad and an armored vehicle parking lot. On Wednesday morning, September 25, Matthews screamed at them to clear the field. They did, and that Friday night, Central High beat the visiting team from Istrouma, Louisiana, and extended its winning streak to twenty-four games.

Billy Moore, quarterback and captain of the Central High Tiger team in 1957 and later All-American quarterback at the University of Arkansas, spoke of Matthews as a great teacher and a great coach, "a modern-day Knute Rockne." Moore recalled how Matthews' pre-game and half-time pep talks could "get young people to give their maximum effort better than any coach I ever knew."

On September 23, two days before the 101st arrived, Matthews gave his team a different type of pre-game talk. The Governor had removed the National Guard and a mob was assembled outside Central High. He called a meeting of his varsity players and gave them this ultimatum: "Don't look out the window and worry about what's going on outside. If I hear of any of you getting involved in any of this, you are finished with football. You will answer to me."[109]

> Coach Matthews said he expected a great deal of trouble at the start of the school year. He instructed us, as only he could, we were not to participate in any activities that would reflect negatively on our team or school if we wanted to play football for him. No exceptions! Who you were didn't matter. Starter or goat, you would not play. I was not going to be part of any activity that would cause the lost of his respect and exclude me from playing football for him. That was just not an option.
>
> Art Pearrow, Class of 1958

Central High football players' respect for Matthews was reflected in the negative reaction one former team member had upon seeing the 1980 docudrama *Crisis at Central High*. In that film, student rabble-rousers were shown wearing letterman's jackets. "That would not have happened" said Ladd Davies, a two-year Tiger football letterman, who remembered Matthews' and other coaches' insistence that athletes stay out of trouble. Davies knew that no one wearing a letterman's jacket would have dared to be a rabble-rouser "because they would have been removed from the team immediately."[110]

Lawrence Mobley: Head Basketball Coach

In 1947, Lawrence "Larry" Mobley had been a starter on Central High's state championship basketball team. In 1957, with Mobley now Head Coach, the team again won the state title. In two other years, his teams were one game short as runners-up. Mobley also served as faculty sponsor for the Key Club, the men's leadership group, which had over one hundred members. Bill Hicks, president of the Key Club that year, recalled the man who strongly inspired him.

> Having just retired from forty-three years of coaching, I can attest to the very positive influence Coach Mobley had on my life, both as one of his "boys" in basketball and in the Key Club, the finest service organization at Central. Coach Mobley had the two best qualities of any coach—tough discipline and tough love—and has been recognized as a great coach. He also spent many extra hours helping us plan programs, get speakers like Colonel Koonce of the 101st Airborne, and sponsor Homecoming and Thanksgiving food baskets for the less fortunate.
>
> Bill Hicks, Class of 1958

Mobley and other Central High coaches helped maintain school discipline and security. During the numerous bomb scares phoned in almost daily during September and October 1957, Mobley and other coaches checked hall lockers. Like other coaches, he was also stationed in the halls during the five-minute class breaks and in the cafeteria to help maintain calm and order.

Clyde Hart: Head Track Coach and Trainer

Before he became a high school and college track coach, Clyde Hart was an Arkansas high school and Baylor University track star, setting state, university, and NCAA records. As Central High's head track and cross-country coach for six years, his teams won state titles in both sports every year but one, 1958-59, when all Little Rock public high schools were closed. And even in that year, Hart's influence produced a champion.

149

Central High Track team member and state record holder Glynn Fields took a detailed workout schedule Hart had prepared for him when he transferred to a school in Georgia. Fields said that because of his former coach's training program, he became the high point scorer in the Georgia State Track Meet and the Outstanding Track Athlete among Georgia high schools in 1959.

Hart remained at Central High until 1963, when he became head track coach at Baylor University in Waco, Texas, a position he held for the next forty-two years. One of the most successful coaches in track history, Hart's accomplishments include coaching four Olympic Gold Medalists, ten world record holders, eight national collegiate record holders, and an astonishing 474 All-Americans.

Portions of Hart's story of Central High in 1957 are told here in his own words:[111]

> After graduating from Baylor, I worked for awhile as a roughneck in the oil fields in Wink, Texas. In late May or early June 1957, my father told me that Central High was looking for a new track coach. I met with Superintendent Blossom, who told Principal Matthews he had hired me. Nothing was mentioned in my interview about integration. I had no knowledge of the pending desegregation plan at Central or what was about to happen. When I met with Matthews, he didn't mention anything either.
>
> During summer football practice, I remember Principal Matthews told the football team he didn't know what to expect when school started. But he asked the team, as he had already asked us coaches, if they saw any problem to step in and help stop it. He had great confidence that the leaders at Central High would do the right thing.
>
> Principal Matthews called the coaches in and said they had gotten a bomb threat. He wanted us to check

the lockers, which we did without even thinking. In those days, the idea that somebody would put a bomb in the school was so absurd, we thought the possibility of that happening was very slim. But we had to be able to say we checked the lockers. I can remember opening lockers, lifting up brown sack lunches, books and papers, with no idea about booby-trapping.

One morning after the 101st took control, they brought this guy in to the first-aid station they had set up in the gym. He had a big gash above his eye and his head was bloody. The soldiers just patched him up; then they let him go. The story was this guy stood in front of a paratrooper and spit on him and cussed him. The paratrooper never blinked an eye, but the guy ignorantly reached out and touched the trooper's piece. When he did that, he was immediately struck in the head with the butt of the M-1 rifle. That was the only real injury I remember due to the turmoil, which in itself is remarkable.

The 101st parked their half-tracks on the track and did quite a bit of damage. But the worst part was they burned some of our old wooden hurdles because it was cold. We had to get new ones. The school athletic director said I would have to raise the money myself to replace them. I wrote a letter to President Eisenhower, complaining about the treatment of the track and particularly about burning up our hurdles. We got a reimbursement check that allowed us to do some work on the track and to replace the hurdles. Also, I got a nice reply from the President. That changed me from a Democrat to a Republican right there.

The students at Central High, the faculty, and everybody involved at school should be credited for their poise and discipline under those conditions. To my knowledge, no injuries were reported inside Central that year. In fact, while the youngsters called the Little Rock Nine are cited as heroes, I think the Central faculty and student body were equally heroes in their own right. Those mobs and bomb scares threatened everybody inside Central, not just the Little Rock Nine.

Many teachers were harassed at home for just doing their job and not openly defying the court decision. The faculty and students, black and white, were equally heroes. Those black kids had to walk through that line, but once they were in the building, every student was treated the same as far as the teachers were concerned.

Clyde Hart, Head Track Coach

Voices From Central High: National Guardsmen and Airborne Troops

The paratroopers stood almost shoulder-to-shoulder armed with M-1s and bayonets in the middle of the streets surrounding the school. The segregationist mob soon discovered the paratroopers would respond to personal attacks by swinging the butt of a rifle against the assailant's head.

Joe Matthews, Class of 1958

Since this time frame was before most buildings were air-conditioned, classroom windows remained open a good bit of the time. I'll never forget the day in our English class when Miss Piercey stopped leading our group and had us listen to what was going on outside. A group from the 101st was marching around the school, singing a normal cadence of theirs which contained inappropriate language. Miss Piercey was incensed and went directly down to the office to report it to Mr. Matthews. I don't know who talked to the commander, but there were no more lyrics sung during school hours while the guys were marching.

Margaret Johnson Swaty, Class of 1958

I remember hearing "Here they come," and I saw black students coming down the street escorted by our troops. The other students showed up and went to school, wondering what all the fuss was about. I felt

153

they were relieved to see federal troops in place of the National Guard. I didn't see or experience any of the media's "reported" problems from any of the students. What was "not real" was blown out of proportion, and what was "real" was very calm and efficient.

During the fifty-six days that I spent in Little Rock, the students and local Little Rock citizens treated me and my fellow troopers with respect and dignity. The most fulfilling memory I have is one of seeing the smiles on the faces of the children from St. Joseph's Orphanage during the Halloween Party that we put on for them at Camp Robinson.

Chuck Christman, 1st Airborne Battle Group,
327th Infantry, 101st Airborne Division

The day school opened, it was interesting to see the National Guard troops on the campus. There were several of them who had graduated from Central only three months earlier and who had planned to go to college about this time. Here they were, on active duty in front of some of their friends from the previous school year. We made fun of them and it was a relaxed atmosphere. There was no discipline among the National Guard members and it was more of a circus atmosphere. Everything was very casual.

Craig Rains, Class of 1958

I do remember the Arkansas National Guard troops standing around, seemingly without a mission or a leader, and thinking that we might be in for some tough times if we were counting on them to defeat the Red Menace. However, they were friendly and did not cause any harm.

Later they were replaced by the 101st Airborne and I remember thinking this was the real reason the Russians had not tried to invade us. Those guys were fit and ready to handle any task their commander assigned to them.

Charles Oakley, Class of 1958

Chapter 5

The Burden of Ethics

Afterwards, my Dad [former Mayor Mann] rarely discussed the Little Rock crisis—primarily because he felt so bitter. He was a native Arkansan who loved the state of Arkansas. He felt he did what he was morally required to do, and he was vilified by the people of his home state because of the courageous stand he took.

Woody Mann, Class of 1958

In every political event, three groups of people can be identified: those who make decisions affecting others—elected or appointed officials; those who implement those decisions—bureaucrats and administrators; and those affected by the decisions—the general public.

Each group is responsible only for its own actions, although those actions may profoundly affect the lives of others. And in the democratic process, each group is free to express dissatisfaction with its assigned tasks. As necessary, each group may also modify the outcomes of its task. The democratic system works very well when all participants accept their roles with decorum. Central High students, it should be remembered, were prohibited from any school discussion and had little opportunity to modify their assigned task of not getting involved.

Fear and pride are the fundamental human emotions that most frequently cause the system to break down. These powerful emotions can overwhelm the best intentions and transform a prescribed and proven process into chaos. Citizens have a responsibility to resist those forces, to balance negative influences with a larger understanding of what is good for themselves and for society, to keep focused on a goal, and to conduct themselves accordingly. This is the burden of ethics, the price that must be paid for doing what is good and what is right.

157

The burden of ethics challenged two particular groups with varying tasks of either making ethical decisions or implementing those decisions in everyday life. On one end of the spectrum was the U.S. Supreme Court, which ruled against "separate but equal" schools and expected local response with "all deliberate speed." The Supreme Court had complete responsibility for making the large decisions in *Brown* and *Brown II* but no responsibility for implementing them. On the other end of the spectrum, Central High administrators, teachers, and students had no opportunity to make large decisions that affected others, but they bore the greatest burden in accepting and assimilating into their lives the decisions made by others.

Central High students, in particular, had the challenging role of accepting decisions made by others, and the burden of ethics was heavy on their shoulders. Adults of authority or influence—school board members, teachers, and parents—had each given Central High students a set of choices, often a conflicting set.

The students could accept the planned change and its accompanying unknown uncertainties, which most did, and gain the approval of the school authorities, teachers, parents, and ministers. Many students accepted the planned changes of desegregation and, in the process, showed friendship to the blacks. They were surprised that their actions put them at risk of violent opposition and social ostracism from other quarters.

Alternately, students could reject the planned changes proposed by school authorities. A few of them, with the backing of their parents and ministers, chose to do so. Their efforts, to disrupt school, to oppose desegregation, and to regain the familiar environment of racial segregation gained them approval of highly visible and vocal segregationist groups within the community. They received only limited disapproval or sanction from other quarters.

Students who made either choice could also publicly vocalize in the news media their support or opposition to the planned changes. Those public statements often caused the students regret. Most students simply put their decisions quietly into action in very private ways.

Doing Good for the Wrong Reasons

I am so angry and offended that my mother and father and other adults I grew up around kept saying we had to desegregate because "it's the law" instead of "it's the right thing to do!" I am even more offended at the adults who continued to support segregation and intimidated everybody else.

Ladd Davies, Class of 1958

In a simple world where our motives are pure and our actions uncomplicated, we can hold people accountable to the highest standards of behavior. In that idealistic realm, obeying the law, in itself, would not merit praise, would not qualify as a good or moral action unless it was based on a fundamental belief that the law itself was good. In that world, where the morality of the law is assumed good and never questioned, a person who obeyed the law for any other reason, such as just following orders, would be doing good for the wrong reason.

Conversely, it is possible to do wrong for a good reason. In Victor Hugo's *Les Miserables*, a character steals bread because he is unable to feed his children. His crime is theft, for which he is severely punished. The tragedy of that story is that the law has no compassion for the human condition. The law is held as an objective and abstract truth which people must accept or pay a dear consequence.

At Central High, the core motive behind many persons' decisions was to obey the law. Most teenagers in that era had been taught to believe the law, in whatever form it took, was good and moral. They subordinated personal values, such as disagreement with school desegregation or personal ideas about black people. But others put their personal beliefs above the law and felt morally compelled to interfere.

When *New York Times* reporter Benjamin Fine sat on the bus station bench beside Elizabeth Eckford and gently encouraged her with the words, "Don't let them see you cry," he violated the unofficial rule of his profession to keep an objective distance from his subject. Does that momentary act of kindness disqualify him as a credible reporter?

159

Similarly, respect for General Edwin Walker, commander of the 101st Airborne Division, may be compromised because five years later the general, then retired, was arrested for sedition as the ringleader of riots on the campus of the University of Mississippi in an effort to block the entrance of its first black student, James Meredith. Despite his personal feelings about black and white children attending school together in Little Rock in 1957, Walker obeyed the President, his commander-in-chief, in an exacting fashion.[112] His private decisions in Mississippi clearly contradicted his earlier military decisions at Central High.

Mayor Mann, one of the city's strongest advocates for the rule of law, offers another example of this self-subordination.

> Probably the most amazing thing is that, privately, my dad never supported classroom integration, nor did he support the 1954 U.S. Supreme Court decision which made school segregation unconstitutional. However, as he told me time and time again, as the Mayor of Little Rock, he had taken an oath to uphold the Constitution of the United States, regardless of his personal feelings.
>
> Woody Mann, Class of 1958

In some cases, as with some members of the 1957-58 Little Rock School Board, personal views opposing integration were expressed, presumably as a demonstration of the compromise that those persons were willing to accept to uphold the law. The disclaimer, of course, can also be used as a personal defense against retaliation, a type of self-vindication that suggests "I disagree with the ruling, but I voluntarily accept a citizen's duty to uphold it."

This approach was included in a public letter by several dozen Little Rock attorneys printed shortly before the September 27, 1958 special election to decide whether or not to close the schools. The attorneys urged citizens to face frankly the "hard alternatives and preserve free public education" by accepting integrated schools. They also wrote "...a limited integrated school system pursuant to court orders is distasteful to many in our group, but the alternative of no public school system is even more distasteful."[113]

160

The choice, presented here as the lesser of two evils, did not convince Little Rock voters in September 1958, who voted nearly two-to-one for closing city public high schools.

The final questions, therefore, should not be: Who wanted school desegregation, who agreed it was a good thing, who ethically embraced the ideas behind the Supreme Court's *Brown* decision? The number of people in Little Rock in that group was probably extremely small.

More appropriately, the questions should be phrased: Who accepted the school board's decision to comply with the law and the school desegregation that went with it, who conducted themselves in a manner to allow its success, and who, for whatever reason, did the right thing?

Piety and Self-Righteousness

That I came out of Central High on the right side of history is something for which I deserve little credit, while my parents deserve much. I don't remember why I was once called a "N**** lover." I would be prouder of myself today if that had happened more often.

Elaine Emanuel Whitaker, Class of 1960

On September 5, 1957, Mayor Mann charged that Faubus' claim of threatened violence in the public schools was a "disgraceful political hoax" that could retard state progress for more than twenty-five years if it were not stopped. In retrospect, Mann's comments, like the rough language Coach Matthews used with his championship football team, seem refreshingly candid and true.

Mann challenged Faubus because the Governor did not fulfill his constitutional duty to uphold the law as determined by the courts. To counter all opposition, Faubus drew a self-defining circle and placed his opposition outside, implying that "you're either for us or against us." The ability to categorize and dramatically distinguish opposite positions is a powerful political tool.

In the fall of 1957, moral lines were quickly and rigidly drawn. Liberal media and integrationists, for example, believed if you had any reservation about desegregation, integration, or civil rights, regardless of the merit, you were a "racist." But segregationists believed if you were not totally against integration in its every manifestation, and specifically the school board's plan for minimal desegregation, you were for it and therefore an "integrationist" to be reviled. Seldom is any complex social issue that simple or clear cut.

The quest for the simplest statement of belief created self-righteous positions and one-word slogans. In this atmosphere, no "moderate" position was allowed in public discourse without attacks from both extreme sides. In the fall of 1958, Little Rock School Board member Dr. Dale Alford defeated nine-term Congressman Brooks Hayes in the 2nd District of Arkansas. Alford capitalized on Hays' "moderate" position on integration during the Central High segregation crisis. Reducing the issue to its ultimate simplicity, Alford declared the "moderate" position to be treasonous to the South.[114]

Based on commentary in 1997 at the fortieth anniversary program at Central High, questions can be raised whether Alford's assessment has ever changed. A guest editorial by Wesley Pruden, a Little Rock native who became editor-in-chief of the *Washington Times*, offered a scathing review of the pious and self righteous rhetoric expressed at that ceremony.[115] Titled "Holier than thou week down home," Pruden wrote of Mike Huckabee, then-Governor of Arkansas, calling white parents of that earlier era "evil," and President Clinton comparing Orval Faubus and his followers to the butchers of Bosnia.

"The white merrymakers," Pruden, son of a Little Rock clergyman who led segregationist rallies and decried the "mongrelization of the races," continued, "want everyone to remember how noble they were when everyone else was bad." Pruden wrote that he "was there as a young reporter, and it didn't happen that way. …. The resisting white parents were wrong, but they were neither 'morally corrupt' nor 'Satanic'…they were men and women imprisoned in their own time and experience. If there was a white man in all of Arkansas who thought desegregation was actually good, it was hard to find him."

National Park Service Superintendent Michael Madell described the events at outside Central High as "not a chapter of history that reflects very well on the white community here in Little Rock. We can't change what occurred fifty years ago."[116] That position is echoed in the reflections of Woody Mann, the mayor's son.

I often wondered later, where were the other public officials, the ministers, and all the good people of Little Rock who should have said "This is our town and you're not going to do this in a city that we love." Instead, for the most part, my Dad carried that banner—or cross—by himself.

Woody Mann, Class of 1958

History cannot be changed, but the telling of history should be understood for its potential as propaganda or subjectivity. The origins of propaganda are not always sinister. They can be as simple as the unquestioned retelling of rumors, such as the *Arkansas Democrat*'s reporting of fights occurring inside Central High when that did not occur. Or propaganda may occur when a historian tries to create balance by introducing new information.

History, some believe, says more about the time in which it is written than the time it describes. Particularly when analyzing highly controversial subjects, one can only show how certain opinions came to be held. The most honest historian provides information and analysis that allows an audience the chance to draw its own conclusions as it observes the prejudices, beliefs, and perspectives of the speaker.

The Search for Heroes

The intensity of analytical historical rhetoric gets even higher when the word "heroes" is used. Basic definitions of the word use terms such as "nobility," "courage," "daring," and "self-sacrifice." Heroism is generally shown through action. One cannot be heroic without actively doing something. Heroism can also be shown by enduring oppression.

One of the Little Rock Nine was so very, extremely shy. For her I felt so bad, because I could identify with her shyness, and I ached for her and for how this all affected her.

Dorothy Hawn Larch, Class of 1959

163

These words exhibit compassion, a highly admirable trait that can be an impetus to heroism. But without doing something to act upon her feelings, this student would not be considered heroic.

A perceived lack of action elicited statements from journalists at the former *Arkansas Democrat*, who, in 1980, wrote that the only heroes of the integration crisis at Central High were black, and that published accounts of the events, notably Huckaby's book, dispelled any notions the journalists might have had about heroic whites at the school.[117] Twenty five years later, similar editorial views continued to be printed in local newspapers.

While Central's faculty and student body successfully confronted one of America's greatest social challenges since the Civil War, none claim to be heroes. None seek any historical parity with the Little Rock Nine or others whose beliefs were dramatically tested and whose lives were repeatedly threatened. No comparisons of heroics or bravery are appropriate because everyone who stepped inside Central High that year exhibited courage every day—some more than others.

Clyde Hart confirms that Central High's nine black students were "heroes in what they did," but he strongly contends that the faculty and students were also heroes.

> The Little Rock Nine were made heroes because they were in a dangerous situation, but they were not isolated from the student body. You can't tell me if there had been a bomb in that building, that bomb would have only killed the black students. They went through harassment to get into the building; but a lot of the white kids were cussed at for just going into school, too, and others were cussed at for being friendly to the black students after they got to school.
>
> Clyde Hart, Head Track Coach

Hart's direct language in praise of his students can be compared to the message Principal Matthews wrote to the senior class in the 1958 school yearbook. Matthews' formal words expressed a sense of heroic behavior in the students for their overall response to the atten-

164

tion that was on them. "The graduating Class of 1958 will always stand out in my memory," Matthews wrote, "because the class as whole reacted so admirably to the shock of having the eyes of the world focused on the school, ... and the class united in a very cooperative way to leave a fine record of achievement at Central."

Hart and Matthews certainly were proud of the young people at their school. Their words reflect that emotional tie to the students. On another level, their message to them speaks to the truthfulness of any story, how what is told about Central High or anywhere depends on the eyes and heart of the reporter. Reporting will also be influenced by a person's proximity to the events, his truthfulness in reporting, as well as his reason for being present at all, and his reward for reporting history accurately, fabricating the next hot story, or supporting a politically correct belief.

Preach a Little Love

From an academic and athletic perspective, the 1957-58 school year at Central High was successfully completed, and a final newspaper headline could proclaim: "School Integrated, Not Much Else Happens."

Though it wasn't a normal school year, in every normally measurable way, it was a highly successful school year. Yet individual lives were changed, and the direction of a national struggle with racial equity changed with them. Those changes continue, defying efforts in the search for closure, a term often used by a society that wants to get on with things and not linger on difficult feelings or emotions.

But closure can also mean a process by which the pain of the past can be transformed into a foundation for healing and growth in the future. Larry Taylor, Pastor Emeritus at Emmanuel Baptist Church, Alexandria, Louisiana, has struggled with closure for decades. As a member of the "Lost Class" of 1959, Taylor was denied his senior year at Central High, and he graduated from Sylvan Hills High School in North Little Rock. For him, Central High is still an open wound. On return trips to Little Rock, he finds himself driving by the school and looking for something he says he is not sure of.

The Central High experience was the beginning of a change in the way I thought about race and privilege. I grew up through that year of 1957-58. In the years that followed as a pastor, I have tried to make a difference where I had influence. And although we have come a long way as a society, the heart is a distant place, and is still far from home.

Somewhere in his writings William Faulkner identifies the racism of his day as a problem in the hearts of people. Like most evils, one suspects the heart is the host. Something has to happen in people's hearts, the place where attitudes are formed, before anything changes, and for that kind of transformation, nothing works better than understanding and compassion.

I think of my Latin teacher's words that fall morning, nearly fifty years ago. "Preach a little love," she said. And that is what I have tried to do.

Larry Taylor, Class of 1959

Closure

The words remain long after the people who spoke them are gone. Words such as "good citizens" and "rule of law" have uncomplicated meanings. Other words, such as "heroism" or "appropriate behavior" are more complex. In some cases, interpretation of the terms has changed over the decades. Words such as "integration" and "segregation" are understood differently today than they were fifty years ago.

Many aspects of society have changed over the decades. As a nation and as individuals we are more responsive to, and less forgiving of, acts of intolerance that would have been ignored in the past.

Our full understanding of historical events and the people who experienced them requires a willingness to hear the messages from that time. The same messages may vary when told by different persons. Each authentic telling has value.

166

The voices from Central High create a third side of the historical story. They are part of an American experience, a national conflict and a coming of age. The time they describe has changed, and many of our values have changed as well. These voices define that time and place and the beliefs that were demonstrated there. They are another part of our national heritage.

Appendices

A.   Selected Photographs

B. Timeline of Desegregation at Little Rock Central High School

C. Teacher and Student Contributors—How Central Found its Voices

D. Teachers Purged in 1959

E. Pentangle Service Board letter

F. Index

G. Chapter Notes

Appendix A

Selected Photographs

Rejection, September 4, 1957: *(Above) Elizabeth Eckford is turned away from Central High by the National Guard while a white student walks onto the campus. (Below) Hazel Massery taunts Eckford as she walks away from the school. Photos by Will Counts, Courtesy of Vivian Counts.*

Reconciliation, September 1997: *Elizabeth Eckford and Hazel Massery at the 40th Anniversary events. Photo by Will Counts, Courtesy of Vivian Counts.*

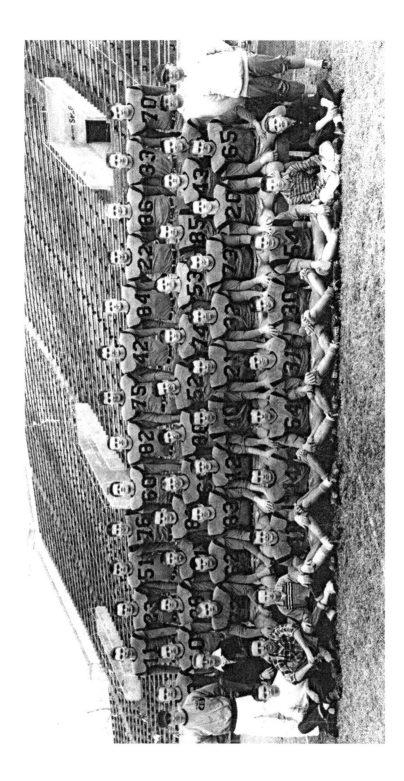

174

Top Team in the Nation: *The 1957 Central High School football team was named the number one team in the nation in 1957 by National Sports News Service of Minnesota. In 2000, a sportswriter listed them as one of the "Twelve Best High School Football Teams in the United States in the Past 100 Years."*

Team Roster: *(Names in bold are students mentioned in Central in Our Lives.)*

Top row: (11) **Ladd Davies** *(Sr. HB); (23) Danny Duggar (Jr. HB); (51) Tom King; (Soph. C) (76) Bill Collier (Jr. T); (60) Buddy Tackett; (Jr. G), (82) Ed Thorne (Sr. E); (75) John Rath (Jr. T); (42)* **Ralph Brodie** *(Sr. QB); (84) Buford Blackwell (Jr. E); (22)* **Bruce Fullerton** *(Sr. HB); (86)* **Bill Hicks** *(Sr. E); (33) Alton (Smitty) Fausett (Sr. FB); (70)* **Art Pearrow** *(Sr. T).*

3rd Row: **Coach Clyde Hart***; (68) Charles Cusick (Soph. T); (10) Bobby Shepherd (Jr. HB); (38) Steve Hathcote (Jr.FB); (61) Alvin Crawford (Jr. G); (81) Charles "Chuck" Patterson (Jr. E); (69) Keneth Zini (Jr. G); (80) Bill Hathcote (Sr. E); (52) Charles Teague (Jr. C); (74) Jerry Pickens (Sr. G); (53)* **Joe Matthews** *(Sr. C); (85) Gilbert Arnold (Sr. E); (43)* **Billy Moore** *(Sr. QB); (77) Ted Blagg (Sr. T);* **Head Coach Wilson Matthew***; Coach Gene Hall*

2nd Row: Henry Mahan (Head Mgr); (72) Bobby Brazzel (Soph. T); (62) Charles Dodd (Soph. G);(83) Larry Dum (Soph. E); (12) Doyne Davis (Jr. HB); (10) Gary Robinson (Soph. HB); (21) Sammy Peters (Sr. HB); (32) Jim Davis (Sr. FB); (73) **Bill May** *(Sr. T); (20 Sam Gill (Sr. HB);Clarence (Bubba) Crist (Jr. G).*

Front Row: John Tate (Soph. Mgr); Bill Shamburger (Soph. Mgr); Jerry McKenney (Soph. Mgr) (41) Fallon Davis (Jr. QB); (14) Jack McClain (Jr. HB); (64) Jim Penn (Sr. G); (31) Ronnie Holmes (Soph. HB);(30) John McCarty (Soph. FB) (54) Darrell Collier (Jr. Center); Bill Tidmore (Soph. Mgr); Jerry McNabb (Soph. Mgr).

Photo courtesy of Jack McClain.

175

Schoolyard Arms: *Rifles of the Arkansas National Guard are positioned while the troops are at rest. Photo courtesy of Bettman/Corbis.*

Military Escort: *The Little Rock Nine enter Central High School escorted by troops of the 101st Airborne Division on September 25, 1957. Photo courtesy of Bettman/Corbis.*

Posing for the Camera: *A widely distributed image purportedly shows unauthorized persons being turned away from Central High school grounds. Several students and a witness to the event describe it as a posed and paid-for photograph. Photo courtesy of* Arkansas Democrat-Gazette.

Among Friends: *Minnijean Brown Trickey (above photo) and Terrance Roberts (below photo) chat with fellow students during a bomb-threat building evacuation on September 26, 1957. Photos by Will Counts, Courtesy of Vivian Counts.*

Solo Walk: *Ernest Green walks unaccompanied at the Central High graduation while white male and female students walk together. Jane Prather (right) walks ahead of Green, her offer to accompany him in the ceremony was declined by school officials who feared a disruption would ensue. Photo courtesy of* Arkansas Democrat-Gazette.

Graduation Day, 1958: *Ken Reinhardt (right) and Ernest Green in graduation robes at Quigley Stadium. Photo courtesy of* Arkansas Democrat-Gazette.

179

More than a Spelling Error: *A sign with a spelling error was placed in front of the closed Central High School in the fall of 1958. The message on the sign was also incorrect, as the school closing was a result of state and local decisions. Photo courtesy of* Arkansas Democrat-Gazette.

Community Response: *CROSS (bottom photo on facing page) and STOP (this page) were opposing community initiatives formed after the firing of Little Rock educators in May 1959. Both conducted active public campaigns for a school board recall election. Photos courtesy of* Arkansas Democrat-Gazette.

Appendix B

Timeline of Desegregation at Little Rock Central High School

A chronological review of the events at Central High warrants comparison to the concept of the "perfect storm." Instead of the convergence of several weather systems at a single moment, the social and political confrontations that occurred in Little Rock were most dramatically played out over a three-year period in 1957-59.

This timeline offers a brief navigational tool to assist in recognition of milestone events in that period. This intense time was the result of a long preceding period when Southern values were shaped and embedded in people's lives. In rural areas, and particularly in the South, cultural values and deeply held beliefs are slow to change.

A three-year whirlwind introduced change that was resisted or embraced by various segments of the community. None of the players acted alone, none weathered the storm without influencing others, and none emerged unchanged.

To understand the full picture of what happened that year, the 1957-58 school year at Little Rock Central High School should be looked at in terms of what happened in Arkansas prior to that year, during it, and immediately afterwards. The dates and events listed below provide a brief glimpse into the key events of those years and a limited mapping of that complex process.

Desegregation Timeline

May 14, 1954—The U.S. Supreme Court decrees that "separate is inherently unequal" in *Brown vs. Board of Education*.

May 22, 1954—The Little Rock School Board agrees to comply with the Supreme Court's decision on school desegregation.

May 24, 1955—The school board adopts Superintendent Virgil Blossom's plan of gradual integration to start in September, 1957 at the high school level and add the lower grades over the next six years. Blossom is named "Man of the Year" by the *Arkansas Democrat* for his work on desegregation.

May 31, 1955—In *Brown II*, the Supreme Court decrees that public school segregation must be ended "with all deliberate speed" but sets no deadlines.

January 28, 1956—Faubus reports that "85% of all people" in Arkansas opposed school desegregation in a statewide poll he commissioned in November.

Spring, 1957—Eighty of the 517 black students who live in the Central High district express interest in attending the school in the fall. Seventeen are selected for the first year of integration. Eight of those decide to remain at all-black Horace Mann High School.

April 30, 1957—Capital Citizens' Council organizes letter writing campaign to Governor Orval Faubus against desegregation of public schools and distributes over 100,000 copies.

Summer, 1957—A welcoming and orientation program for all new students is discussed by Central High Student Council officers.

Mid-August, 1957—Student Council finalizes plan for program for the new black students, tentatively scheduled for August 30th at principal's discretion.

August 23, 1957—Mother's League of Central High School organized.

August 27, 1957—A member of the Mothers' League files a motion seeking a temporary injunction against school integration. Faubus is the only witness and speaks of potential for violence at the school.

August 29, 1957—Pulaski County Chancellor Murray Reed grants the injunction "on the grounds that integration could lead to violence."

August 30, 1957—The first Student Council program for new black students is cancelled by Principal Matthews for safety reasons.

August 30, 1957—Federal District Judge Ronald Davies nullifies the injunction filed by the Mothers' League.

September 2, 1957—Faubus calls out the Arkansas National Guard to preserve the peace and avert violence at Central High.

September 3, 1957—FIRST DAY OF SCHOOL. Judge Davies orders desegregation to start the next day.

September 3, 1957—Mike Wallace calls school and asks to talk with the student body president. Interviews Ralph Brodie.

September 4, 1957—The eight black students attempt to enter Central High but are turned away by the National Guard. Elizabeth Eckford attempts to enter Central High and is also turned away by the National Guard and taunted in the historic picture.

September 5, 1957—Student Council places plans for program on hold until black students' entrance date is settled.

September 17, 1957—Mike Wallace interview with Ralph Brodie is printed in the *Arkansas Gazette*.

September 19, 1957—First issue of *The Tiger*, Central High's student newspaper, is printed. Editorial written by co-editor Jane Emery Prather, asks students, "Can you meet the Challenge?" "...Today the world is watching you, the students of Central High..."

September 20, 1957—Judge Davies rules that Faubus used the troops to prevent integration, not to preserve law and order as he claimed. The Governor removes the National Guardsmen, and the Little Rock Police Department takes over.

September 23, 1957—Nine black students enter Central High through a side door. When the crowd outside becomes unruly, before noon, the black students are removed from the building.

September 24, 1957—Little Rock Mayor Woodrow Mann sends President Eisenhower a telegram asking for federal troops to maintain order and complete the integration process. The President sends 1,000 members of the 101st Airborne Division to Little Rock. He federalizes the 10,000-man Arkansas National Guard.

September 25, 1957—FIRST FULL DAY OF CLASSES FOR LITTLE ROCK NINE. Under escort by the 101st Airborne "Screaming Eagles," the nine black students enter Central High. General Edward A. Walker, chief of the Arkansas Military District controlling the 101st Airborne, addresses student body at assembly.

September 26, 1957—During a fire drill for a false bomb threat, black students Minnijean Brown, Terrance Roberts, and Elizabeth Eckford are photographed by the news media in casual conversation and laughing with white classmates.

September 27, 1957—Student Council welcoming program for black students is cancelled.

October 1, 1957—The 101st turns over student escort service to federalized National Guard.

November 11, 1957—The 101st leaves the building entirely.

November 28, 1957—The federalized National Guard are removed from inside the building.

December, 1957—Taunted by white male students, Brown drops a bowl of chili on her antagonists in the cafeteria. Though she says it was accidental, she is suspended for six days.

February 6, 1958—Following additional altercations with white students, Brown is suspended for the remainder of the school year. She transfers to New Lincoln High School in New York City.

May 27, 1958—Ernest Green becomes the first black student to graduate from Central High.

August, 1958—Faubus calls a special session of the state legislature to pass a law allowing him to close public schools to avoid integration and to lease the closed schools to private school corporations.

September 12, 1958—LITTLE ROCK PUBLIC HIGH SCHOOLS CLOSED. In *Aaron vs. Cooper*, the Supreme Court rules that Little Rock must continue with its integration plan. The school board announces the city's high schools will open on September 15. Governor Faubus orders Little Rock's high schools closed.

September 16, 1958—The Women's Emergency Committee to Open Our Schools is formed and asks for a special election to keep the schools open.

September 27, 1958—Voters oppose integration by a vote of 19,470 to 7,561, voting to close Little Rock's public high schools.

September, 1958—With public high schools in Little Rock closed for the year, more than 750 whites enroll in T. J. Raney High School. Others leave town or the state to continue their educations. A number of black high school students do not attend school anywhere.

September, 1958—The school board leases the city's four high schools to the Little Rock Private School Corp. Within hours, the 8th U.S. Circuit Court of Appeals restrains the School Board from turning over the schools to the private body. The U.S. Supreme Court declares the Supreme Court's 1954 *Brown vs. Board of Education* ruling "the supreme law of the land" and forbids "evasive schemes for segregation."

December 28, 1958—Faubus is ranked in the No. 10 spot in the Gallup Poll's annual list of "The Ten Men in the World Most Admired by Americans."

May 5, 1959—Segregationist members of the school board fire forty-four teachers and administrators suspected of integrationist sympathies. The three moderates on the board walk out, refusing to participate.

May 8, 1959—Stop This Outrageous Purge (STOP) is formed to recall the segregationist members of the board.

May 16, 1959—In response, segregationists organize CROSS (Committee to Retain Our Segregated Schools)

May 25, 1959—STOP wins the recall election, the three segregationists are replaced by moderates on the School Board, and teachers are rehired.

June 18, 1959—Federal court declares unconstitutional the law allowing the Governor to close schools. The new school board announces it will reopen the high schools in the fall.

August 12, 1959—Little Rock public high schools reopen. Two of the original Little Rock Nine, Jefferson Thomas and Carlotta Walls, begin their senior years at Central High. Three black girls attend the new Hall High School. Following a segregationist rally at the state Capitol, about 250 people march to Central High to protest. Little Rock police arrest twenty-one, and fire hoses are turned on the remaining crowd.

August-September, 1959—Tear-gas bombs and dynamite are used against property owned by the school administration, the mayor, and the fire chief. Five men are arrested and sentenced to prison terms of three to five years. Prison term for the mastermind of the attacks is commuted by Faubus after a little more than five months.

Fall, 1972—All grades in Little Rock public schools are desegregated.

Appendix C

Teacher and Student Contributors

How Central Found its Voices

To every thing there is a season ...
a time to keep silence, and a time to speak.
Ecclesiastes 3:1, 7

The first stories from students at Central High in 1957-58 were collected in 1998 at the 40th combined reunions of the Central and Hall Classes of 1958. Several Hall High alumni from that era also contributed. This process was coordinated by Janice Shepherd Swint, Central High's student body vice-president, Jane Emery Prather, *Tiger* Co-Editor, and Ralph Brodie.

The request for information asked for a response to the following points:

1. Incidents/experiences/memories that made a significant impact on you.
2. Personal insight or wisdom about this incident/experience/memory.
3. The impact of the events of 1957-58 on your life or your family.
4. Personal experiences not previously discussed you would like to see presented in a book.

Just prior to the 45th reunions of the classes of 1958, 1959, and 1960, letters were sent to members of those classes asking them to write and submit their own Central High stories.

The collected stories were reviewed, and selected comments from them are used in this book. All Central High stories, in their entirety, will be placed on file in 2008 at the Butler Center for Arkansas Studies in Little Rock, Arkansas.

Help Complete the Central High Story

Many Central High stories remain untold. Persons with experiences they wish to contribute for a potential future edition, please contact:

Little Rock Central High Stories—1957-59
c/o The Butler Center for Arkansas Studies
Central Arkansas Library System
100 Rock Street, Little Rock, AR 72201
Phone: (501) 918-3056 • Fax: (501)375-7451
E-mail: arkinfo@cals.lib.ar.us

Contributors

The persons listed below contributed stories, poems, memorabilia, or other pertinent information. This book could not have been written without listening to their voices.

Teachers at Central High 1957-58
Elizabeth "Sissi" Riggs Brandon
Shirley "Micky" McGalin Dunaway
Coach Clyde Hart
Paul Magro
Margaret Dewberry Matson
Coach Lawrence Mobley
Carol Ann Lackey Patterson
Shirley Swaim Stancil

Other interested parties
Gaylon Boshears, Central High Class of 1956
Chuck Christman, 1st Airborne Battle Group, 327th Infantry, 101st Airborne Division
Margaret Mitchell Ross, Central High Class of 1957
Gene Singleton, federalized Arkansas National Guard

Hall High Class of 1958 (Seniors in 1957-58)

Amanda "Toppy" Cameron
Robert Hogg
Ira Lipman
Beth Potter Matthews
Mary White Weeks

Central High Class of 1960 (Sophomores in 1957-58)

Charles "Chuck" Bell
Nancy Brandt
Charles "Chuck" Chappell
Ann Chotard
Willene Langley Hendon
Betty Fleming Hendricks
Carolyn Glover Hirby
Avay Gray Jaynes
Jackie Davis March
Carol MaGouirk Sanders
Jenny Lee Shumate
Paul Redditt
Elaine Emanuel Whitaker

Central High Class of 1959 (Juniors in 1957-58)

Betty Faye Douglass Brumbelow
Polly Garrett Carlson
Gloria Buck Davis
Harrell Davis
Wanda Jean Moon Davis
Ron Deal
Deanna Adair Etheridge
Sherry Daniel Evans
Glynn Fields
Judy Venable Gee
Barbara Jo Norman Griffis
Richard Hall
Judy Green Harbour
Roger Harrison

Jonnafae Shepherd Hewitt
Dorothy Hawn Larch
Mary Ann Rath Marion
Pat Coger Middleton
Charles "Chuck" Patterson
Monika Hartstein Poe
Wendell Ross
David Scruggs
Helen Kingrey Sebren
John Taylor
Larry Taylor
Carolyn Martin Watts
Ann Williams Wedaman
Judith Nahlen Wegman

Central High Class of 1958 (Seniors in 1957-58)

Betty Ann Parsons Adams
Joan Boveia Adcock
Jane Teague Allred
Pat Abel Ashworth
Jo Ellen Clark Barnard
Paul Barnes
Marita Talley Bivins
Ralph M. Brink, Sr.
Barbara Barnes Broce
Ralph Brodie
Linda McNutt Brooks
Peggy McKinnon Thompson Brown
Saundra Dean Callaway
Beach Carre
Betty Jane "B. J." Leggett Chick
Marshall "Skip" Coffman
Edward "Buddy" Cone
Ladd Davies
Alice Harper Curtis Dixon
Lloyd Erickson
A. Smith "Smitty" Fausett

Phil Filiatreau
Charles Evans Forte
Bruce Fullerton
Mary Lee Franklin Friesz
Jim Gee
Pat New Graves
Martha Long Gregory
Henry Griffith
William "Bill" Hathcote
Mary Dougherty Howard
Ron Hubbard
Trudy Levy Jacobson
Glennys Oakes Johns
Mary Blagg Johnson
Lee "Andy" Johnson
Kay Varina Kuehnert Kennedy
Kenneth Koonce
Roy Chadwick Kumpe
Sharon McLemore Maple
Justlyn Matlock
Joseph W. "Joe" Matthews
Sonja Gerrald McCauley
Billy Ray Moore
Roberta Martin Moore
Richard L. Narrell
Arnold Norman
Charles Oakley
Sherrie Smith Oldham
Sandra Buck Palmer
Arthur D. Pearrow
George Ann Baldwin Polk
Jane Emery Prather
Craig Rains
Kirby Riffel
Nina Clouette Rowe
Joe Schenke
Lynn Weber Sigmund

Miriam Joseph Smith
Georgia Dortch Sowers
Anne Emerson Steinmetz
Edith Brockinton Garland Stroud
Steve Swafford
Margaret Johnson Swaty
Janice Shepherd Swint
Marian Moore Thomason
Martha Lyn Oathout Thompson
Yvonne Thompson
Helen Ruth Smith Towns
Lou Ellen East Treadway
Dan Tucker
Lauretta Mashburn Underwood
Ronald Vandament
John E. Vise, Jr
James R. "Jim" Wallace
Patricia "Pat" Daunis Wallace

Appendix D

Central High Teachers and Administrators Purged in May 1959

Central High teachers and administrators accounted for thirty of the forty-four people purged in May 1959.

Principals and Administrative Staff

1. Jess W. Matthews, Central High Principal, whose son Joe was in the Class of 1958.
2. J. O. Powell, Vice Principal for Boys
3. Elizabeth Huckaby, Vice Principal for Girls
4. Alice Coffman, Principal's secretary, whose son Skip was in the Class of 1958.
5. Juanita Brietz, Attendance secretary

Teachers:

1. Christine Poindexter, Head of Math Department.
2. Margaret Reiman, Math and Student Council sponsor
3. Helen Conrad, Math and Student Council sponsor
5. Grace Dupree, Home Economics
6. Frances Rudd, Home Economics
7. Abby Foster, Latin
8. Lorine Lee, Latin
9. Orlana Hensley, Student Guidance Counselor
10. Shirley Swaim Stancil, Student Guidance Counselor
11. Harold Deitz, Student Guidance Counselor
12. Irene Harrell, Spanish
13. Pauline Dunn, Biology
14. Harvey Milner, Biology

15. Doris Glenn, English
16. Kathleen Taylor, English
17. Susie West, English
18. Donna Wells, English
19. Ernest Gephart, Industrial Education
20. Nyna Keeton, Distributive Education
21. Jennie Perkins, History
22. Margaret Stewart, History, Social Science
23. Shirley Stewart, Social Science
24. Shirley "Micky" McGalin Dunaway, Speech
25. Cassie Moore, Physical Education

Appendix E

Pentangle Service Board letter

During 1957-58, Vice Principal Elizabeth Huckaby served as faculty sponsor to the Pentangle Service Board, a group composed of ten students—two each from the five service clubs for junior and senior girls. She devised a plan to give students a broader view of integration than was expressed in Little Rock. Huckaby began showing letters received at Central High to the group. The Pentangle Service Board decided it would respond to the letters, and it drafted the following form response.

Dear _____:

We received your letter concerning the Little Rock crisis and sincerely appreciate your interest. We realized that it is inevitable that your comments were based on newspaper reports. We were shocked at them ourselves. Because most of us were inside the school continuing our daily work, we could not observe any of the violence and were therefore unaware of the incidents which have caused you to be alarmed.

The disturbing reports which you received concerned only a small number of our population. The violence was confined to a small area and appears to have been started by those wanting to excite trouble. These acts, unfortunately, were fully reported but did not necessary reflect a true picture of our community.

Because reporters were not allowed in the school, there was little mention of the majority of the students, who objected to violence, regardless of their own opinions. They sought to continue their education in the usual manner, to conduct themselves properly, and to accept the laws of our country. We are writing you, not to deny the unfortunate conflict, but to reveal a clearer picture of the situation.

Today, Central High School represents an ordinary school of our nation. Our educational program has not been changed, and the students continue enjoying their activities such as sports and club organizations. Although the nine Negro students are facing a difficult situation at Central this year, they are attending regularly and progressing in their classes.

In closing, we of Central High School sincerely hope that this letter will help you to form a clearer conception of our actions. What the world needs now is the "peace that passes all understanding"; many students at Central are working toward that peace. Although problems arise, we must all forever strive for peace throughout the world and understanding between people and nations.

_____, Secretary.
Pentangle Service Board

Appendix F

Index

101st Airborne Division... 26, 36, 37, 41, 57, 61, 68, 75, 85, 93, 98, 99, 101, 129, 133, 145, 147, 149, 151, 153, 154, 160

ABC-TV 67

Adams, Betty Ann Parsons 43

Alexandria, Louisiana. 165

Alford, Dale 162

Allred, Jane Teague 104

American Bandstand 30

American Legion 136, 137

Arkadelphia, Arkansas 97

Arkansas Boys State 136, 137

Arkansas Democrat 22, 36, 46, 61, 63, 72, 117, 141, 163, 164

Arkansas Democrat-Gazette 89, 117, 146

Arkansas Gazette. 28, 64, 67, 81, 103, 113, 116, 117, 130, 145

Arkansas General Assembly
    Legislative Council 109

Arkansas Girls State 136, 137

Arkansas High School Press Association . . 43

Arkansas National Guard. 22, 25, 45, 58, 60, 62, 68, 81, 84, 86, 87-89, 92, 101, 111, 130, 148, 154

Arkansas Power & Light Co. 80

Arkansas State Police 89
    Criminal Investigation Division . 109, 110

Arkansas State Press 117

Arkansas Times. 117

Ashmore, Harry. 81, 116, 117

Associated Press 63, 72

Atlanta, Georgia 50

Baldwin, Deborah 15

Barnard, Jo Ellen Clark 93, 101

Barnes, Everett. 41, 42

Barnes, Paul 54

Barrier, Mike 45

Bass, Madge Gregory. 137

Bates, Daisy 33, 34, 104

Baton Rouge, Louisiana 108, 109

Baylor University. 149, 150

Beebe, Arkansas 71

Bell, Charles E. "Chuck" 33, 35, 37, 129

Bentonville, Arkansas 78

Bill Haley and the Comets 20

Black Panthers 125

Blass Department Store. 81

Blossom, Virgil 46, 54, 72, 80, 84, 102, 108, 109, 121, 150
    Blossom Plan 80

Blossom, Gail. 48, 51, 52, 121, 136, 137

Boshears, Gaylon 61

Boys Nation 137

Bradford, Eddie Bradford 147

Branch, Taylor 35

Brandon, Elizabeth "Sissi" Riggs . . 46, 96, 136

Brandt, Nancy 124

Brietz, Juanita. 185

Brink, Sr., Ralph M. 53, 128

Broce, Barbara Barnes 27, 99, 100, 104

Brodie, Ralph 11, 15, 36, 45, 56, 67-70, 99, 130, 132, 137, 138, 140-142, 144, 145

Brodie, Hazel Gray and Frank T. 142

Brown, Jim. 144

Brown II 80, 84, 158

Brown vs. Board of Education 76, 80, 139, 158, 160

Brucker, Wilbur 57

Byrd, Harry 76

CBS 60

Carre, Beach. 129

Central High School. 11-13, 15, 16, 19, 21-24, 27, 28, 31, 34, 35, 37, 41, 44, 45, 47, 50, 51, 54, 55-58, 60, 62, 63, 68, 74, 75, 80, 81, 83, 95-98, 105-107, 109, 113-118, 122, 131, 132, 134, 136, 145, 157, 158, 163, 165, 166
    Alma Mater 13
    Beta Club 31, 50
    Chapel Club. 38, 99, 102
    Class of 1958 . . . . 29, 30, 132, 165
    Class of 1959 . . . . 106, 107, 165
    Debonaires 50
    High Steppers 125

Key Club 31, 50, 55, 149
National Honor Society 50
Opening and name change 131
Pentangle Service Club 45
Southernaires 50
Student Council 48-50
Welcoming Program 48, 49
Chancellor, John 63, 65
Chappell, Charles 28
Charleston, Arkansas 78
Chick, Betty Jane "B. J." Leggett . . . 125, 126
Christman, Chuck 154
Citizens' Council 86
    Capital Citizens' Council 37, 46, 77, 82, 83
Civil War 164
Clinger, Major General Sherman 62
Clinton, Bill 136, 137, 162
CNN 31
Coffman, Marshall "Skip" 185
Coffman, Alice 185
Columbia University Graduate School
    of Journalism 44
Communism 74, 75
    Communist Party 109
Conrad, Helen 185
Conway, Arkansas 89
Cope, Graeme 46, 50, 54
Cotham, Ralph 38
Counts, Will 22, 60, 85
Craighead County 143
Crisis at Central High 121
Crist, Bubba 128
CROSS (Committee to Retain Our
    Segregated Schools) 115
Dailey, Jim 30
Davies, Ladd 148, 159
Deal, Ron 61
Deitz, Harold 185
Democratic Party 75
Dixon, Alice Harper Curtis 76
Dunaway, Shirley "Micky"McGalin . . . 32, 49, 111, 186
Dunn, Pauline 185
Dupree, Grace 185
Eighth Circuit Court of Appeals 111
Eisenhower, Dwight D. . . . 25, 57, 64, 72, 73, 75, 85, 88, 151
Elizabeth Eckford . . 22, 31, 32, 60, 62, 81, 97, 98, 124, 130, 159
Emmanuel Baptist Church 165

Erickson, Lloyd . . . 19, 47, 86, 103, 105, 116
Eyes on the Prize 122
Faubus, Orval 12, 68, 75, 78, 86, 88, 109, 111, 117, 130, 138, 140, 161, 162
    The Faubus Years 88
Faulkner, William 166
Fayetteville, Arkansas 78
FBI 99
Feiock, Josephine 133
Fields, Glynn 150
Fifteenth Amendment of the
    U.S. Constitution 76
Filiatreau, Phil 59, 82
Fine, Benjamin 62, 159
Forest Park Elementary School 115
Fort Smith, Arkansas 78
Forte, Charles Evans 23, 26, 71
Foster, Abby 138, 185
Fulbright, J. W. 88
Fullerton, Bruce 121, 137, 145
Gannett Media 117
Gephart, Ernest 186
Glenn, Doris 186
Governor's Mansion 86
Graves, Pat New 57
Gray, John Cleveland 143
Green, Ernest . . . 39-42, 65, 99, 100, 102, 126
Greenberg, Paul 89
Griffin, Marvin 77, 78, 86
Griffis, Barbara Jo Norman 92
Halberstam, David 57, 74, 97, 98
Hall High School . . . 29, 63, 64, 80, 106, 109, 115, 134
Hardie, Dick 27, 38
Harrell, Irene 185
Harris, Alberta 93
Harris, Roy 86
Hart, Clyde 108, 149, 152, 164, 165
Hayes, Brooks 162
Hazel, Helen 98
Heiskell, J. N. 116
Hensley, Orlana 185
Hicks, Bill 39, 137, 145, 149
Hirby, Carolyn Glover 24, 29, 44, 78, 123, 140
Hodges, Luther 77
Holt, Frank 142
Horace Mann High School 80, 81, 106
Hot Springs, Arkansas 78
Hoxie, Arkansas 78
Hubbard, Ron 137

Huckabee, Mike. 162
Huckaby, Elizabeth. . . . 46, 67, 112, 121, 135,
    164, 185
Istrouma High School. 108, 147
Jaynes, Avay Gray. 20, 22, 91
Jim Crow 82
Johns, Glennys Oakes. . . 38, 41, 55, 104, 133
Johnson, James D. 75
Johnson, Lee "Andy" 119
KARK–TV Channel 4 58
KATV–Channel 7. 62
Kartychok, George. 44
Keeton, Nyna. 186
Kennedy, John F. 136
Kennedy, Kay Varina Kuehnert 34
Ku Klux Klan 81
Lape, A. L. 133
Larch, Dorothy Hawn. 73, 106, 139, 163
Lee, Lorine 185
Les Miserables. 159
Life Magazine 53
Lipman, Ira 63-65
Little Rock, Arkansas 16, 78, 79, 82, 96,
    105, 116, 163
    Chamber of Commerce 115
    City Hall. 25, 82
    Council of Churches. 50
    Hillcrest area 116
    Private School Corporation. 111
    School Board 33, 46, 71, 72, 80, 84,
        89, 107-109, 111, 112, 160
    School District. 107, 112, 135
    Vo-Tech. 80
Little Rock Nine. . . 11, 23, 33, 36, 38, 40, 48,
    49, 54, 56, 63, 68, 89, 92, 96, 100, 105,
    125, 128, 152, 163, 164
Look Magazine 53
Machiavelli. 87
Madell, Michael. 162
Magro, Paul 26, 46, 84, 93, 136, 180
Mann, Woodrow. . . . 81, 82, 84, 85, 103, 109,
    140, 157, 160
Mann, Woody 25, 81, 102, 134, 140, 141,
    157, 160-163
March, Jackie Davis. 27, 105, 107
Marion, Mary Ann Rath . . . 74, 103, 124, 138
Marion County 96
Massery, Hazel Bryan 22, 23
Massive Resistance. 76
Matlock, Justlyn. 28, 29, 137
Matthews, Joseph W. "Joe" . . 22, 49, 102, 153

Matthews, Jess W. 12, 20, 25, 31, 39, 42,
    44, 46, 48, 49, 57, 112-114, 121, 135,
    136, 145, 146, 150, 153, 164, 165, 185
Matthews, Wilson 128, 146-148, 161
May, Bill 125
Mays, Willie 144
McCarthy, Eugene. 74, 87, 109
McCauley, Bill 39
McGee, Frank 59, 64, 65
McHughs, Josh 120
McKinley, Ed I. 113
McRae, Arkansas 71
Meredith, James. 160
Metcalf, Marguerite 63
Michelangelo 15
Middlebrook, Edna 42, 43, 45
Mid-South Opinion Surveys 86
Milner, Harvey. 185
Mississippi 96
Mitchell, William Starr 115
Mobley, Lawrence 148, 149
Monette, Arkansas 143
Monroe, Vaughn 20
Moore, Billy Ray 147
Moore, Cassie 186
Moore, Roberta Martin. 48, 122, 139
Morin, Relman. 72
Moses, Hamilton 80
Mothers' League of Central High School . . 37,
    46, 54, 82, 83
Mothershed, Thelma. 63
NAACP 57
Nalley, Gann 84
Natchez, Mississippi 108
National Council of Churches 50
National Merit Semifinalists. 134
National Park Service 162
National Sports News Service of
    Minnesota. 146
New York Post 147
New Zealand 22
Newsom, Eugene. 87
Newsweek Magazine 53
Nimitz, Admiral Chester 140
North Carolina 77
North Little Rock, Arkansas 165
Oakley, Charles 28, 41, 42, 155
Oldham, Sherrie Smith. 95, 99, 131
Olympic Gold Medalist. 150
Okinawa, Japan 93
Ouachita Baptist University 97

Palmer, Sandra Buck 91
Parker, Sammie Dean 60, 91
Patillo, Melba 99, 104
Patterson, Carol Ann Lackey . . . 100, 110, 135
Pearrow, Arthur D. 58, 62, 144, 148
Pentagon 57
Pentangle Service Club 45
Penton, Emily. 134, 135
Perkins, Jennie 186
Pfeifers Department Store. 81
Piercey, Mary 91, 153
Poindexter, Christine. 185
Powell, J. O. 25, 109, 110, 112, 135, 185
Prather, Jane Emery 21, 36, 43, 46, 67,
    74, 102
Pruden, Wesley. 162
Pulitzer Prize 35, 64, 89, 116
Purge (the Purge of Teachers) 110, 112,
    113, 115, 125
    Declaration by Former Students
    Against 113
Quigley, Earl. 146
Quigley Stadium 39, 98, 145
Rains, Craig 122, 130, 154
Rath, Henry 71, 72, 82, 103
Ray, Gloria 34
Redditt, Paul. 39, 128
Reed, Roy 140
Reiman, Margaret 48, 133, 185
Reinhardt, Ken. 97, 98
Rime of the Ancient Mariner 91
Ripley's Believe It or Not 146
Roberts, Terrance. 39, 63
Rockne, Knute 147
Ross, Wendell. 32, 39, 127, 137
Rudd, Frances 185
Russell, Bill 144
Sanders, Carol MaGouirk. 120
Schakne, Robert. 60
Schmidt, Linda Vassaur 34
Schwartz, Marvin. 15, 16
"Screaming Eagles" 85
Shakespeare 88
Shumate, Jenny Lee. 133
Sigmund, Lynn Weber. 100, 101
"Sixty Minutes" 120
Smith, Gene. 84
Sophocles 88
Southern Manifesto. 27, 75, 76
Sowers, Georgia Dortch 43
Spann, Ronnie 120

Sports Illustrated 120, 128
Stahlkopf, James. 58, 59
Stancil, Shirley Swaim. 19, 51, 112, 185
Stewart, Margaret 46, 47, 186
Stewart, Shirley 186
STOP (Stop This Outrageous Purge) 112, 115
sundown town 71
Swafford, Steve 42
Swaty, Margaret Johnson 20, 61, 99, 102, 153
Swint, Janice Shepherd 131, 136, 137
Sylvan Hills High School 165
T. J. Raney School 111, 112
Taylor, John 134, 135
Taylor, Kathleen 186
Taylor, Larry. . . 39, 83, 92, 118, 138, 165, 166
Taylor, Maxwell D. 57
Terry, Adolphine. 67
The Fifties 74, 97
The New York Times 43, 62, 159
The Race Beat. 60, 64
The Tiger 36, 42-45, 50, 145, 146
Thompson, Yvonne. 79, 95, 96, 122, 123
Till, Emmett. 96
Time Magazine 59, 60
Towns, Helen Ruth Smith. . . . 26, 34, 35, 39,
    47, 98, 137
Trickey, Minnijean Brown . . . 24, 54, 56, 124,
    126
Truman, Harry. 76
U. S. Supreme Court. 11, 12, 33, 70, 72,
    76, 112, 158, 160
United Nations 50
University of Arkansas 15, 108, 113, 147
Upton, Wayne 71, 72, 82, 83, 111
Victor Hugo 159
Vietnam 37
Walker, Maj. Gen. Edwin 36, 147, 160
Wallace, Mike 67-70, 142
Walls, Carlotta 119, 120
Washington Times 162
Wedaman, Ann Williams. 32, 97, 139
Wells, Donna 186
West, Susie 104, 186
West Side Junior High School 84
Westover Hills Presbyterian Church . . 27, 38
Whitaker, Elaine Emanuel. 161
White, Frank. 85
Wilson, Alex. 58, 85
Wink, Texas 150
Women's Emergency Committee. . . . 67, 115
Young, Andrew, An Easy Burden 50

Appendix G

Chapter Notes

Voices From Central High: Students and Teachers

1 Shirley Swaim Stancil, in *Learning Together At Last, Memories Of The Desegregation Of The Arkansas Public School System*, ed. Paul Root, Pete Parks Center for Regional Studies, (Arkadelphia: Ouachita Baptist University, 2005).

Introduction

2 Monica Leas, "Happy Anniversary?", *Arkansas Times*, September 26, 2006.

Voices From Central High: In the Halls

3 The 101st controlled inside Central High for six days, September 25-30, then turned over the role to the federalized National Guard, who assigned only two soldiers per student.

Chapter 1. Making Choices, Choosing Sides

4 Proclamation by Jim Dailey, Little Rock Mayor, July 11, 1998 recognizing the 40th anniversary of the Class of 1958.
5 *Arkansas Democrat*, April 15, 1958.
6 Taylor Branch, *Parting the Waters, America in the King Years 1954-63*, (New York: Simon & Schuster, 1988) 222-223.
7 FBI report signed by Principal Jess Matthews, September 27, 1957.
8 *The Tiger*, Vol. 64, No. 2, Thursday October 3, 1957, page 1.
9 Ibid.
10 Library of Congress video, http://www.centralhigh57.org/movie2.htm.
11 Elizabeth Huckaby, Crisis at Central High: Little Rock 1957-58 (Baton Rouge: LSU Press, 1980), 80.
12 Graeme Cope, "A Thorn in the Side? The Mothers' League of Central High School and the Little Rock Desegregation Crisis of 1957", *Arkansas Historical Quarterly*, Vol. LVII, No. 2, (Summer 1998), 383.
13 1957-58 Student Council officers: Ralph Brodie, President; Janice Shepherd, Vice President; Craig Rains, 12th Grade Representative; and James Chappell, 11th Grade Representative.
14 FBI report, September 13, 1957, signed by Jess W. Matthews.
15 Cope, 382.
16 Cope, 395.
17 Andrew Young, *An Easy Burden: The Civil Rights Movement and the Transformation of America*, (New York: Harper Collins, 1996), 108-109.
18 Stancil.

19 Virgil T. Blossom, *It Has Happened Here* (New York, Harper, 1959), 124.
20 Cope, 387-388.
21 Only 87 names were offered in Federal Court in June 1958; see FBI report by Principal Jess Matthews, September 27, 1957.
22 Cope, 381.
23 *Arkansas Gazette*, Editorial, February 12, 1959.
24 Gene Roberts and Hank Klibanoff, *The Race Beat: The Press, the Civil Rights Struggle, and the Awakening of a Nation* (New York: Knopf, 2006) 156.
25 Ibid. 180.
26 David Halberstam, *The Fifties*, (New York: Villard Books, 1993), 681.
27 Roberts and Klibanoff, 160.
28 Roberts and Klibanoff, 168.
29 Roberts and Klibanoff, 163.
30 Roberts and Klibanoff, 168.
31 Letter from Eisenhower to Lipman, October 17, 1957.
32 In 1995 Lipman, founder and chairman of National Guardsmark, LLC, one of the world's largest security service firms, honored his lifelong friend by establishing The John Chancellor Award for Excellence. The annual award carries a cash prize of $25,000 and is administered by the Columbia University School of Journalism.

Chapter 2. Arkansas and the South

33 Ralph Brodie copy of letters and telegrams between Upton, Rath, and Morin. October 8-10, 1957.
34 Ibid.
35 Ibid.
36 Ibid.
37 Kasey S. Pipes, *Ike's Final Battle: The Road to Little Rock and the Challenge of Equality* (Los Angeles: World Ahead Media, 2007), 257.
38 *Plessy vs. Ferguson*, 1896.
39 Halberstam, 49-59.
40 Executive Order 10730: Desegregation of Central High School (1957), accessed at http://americanradioworks.publicradio.org/features/marshall/ike.html.
41 http://en.wikipedia.org/wiki/Massive_resistance.
42 Arkansas Congressional delegation included Senators John L. McClellan and J. W. Fulbright; Representatives E. C. Gathings, Wilbur D. Mills, James W. Trimble, Oren Harris, Brooks Hays, and W. F. Norrell.
43 *Congressional Record*, 84th Congress Second Session. Vol. 102, part 4 (March 12, 1956). Washington, D.C.: Governmental Printing Office, 1956. 4459-4460.
44 *Arkansas Gazette*, June 5, 1958.
45 Ibid.
46 Editorial, *Arkansas Democrat*, September 2, 1957.
47 Halberstam, 667-690.
48 Counts, 12.
49 Blossom, 22.
50 Halberstam, 667-690.
51 Harry S Ashmore, *Civil Rights And Wrongs: A Memoir Of Race And Politics 1944-1994* (New York: Pantheon Books, 1994), 104.
52 Blossom, 32.
53 Cope.
54 Ibid.

55 Wayne Upton interview, December 29, 1970, Columbia University Dwight D. Eisenhower Administration Oral History Project, 32-33.
56 Ashmore. 114.
57 Elizabeth Jacoway, *Turn Away Thy Son: Little Rock, the crisis that shocked the nation*, (New York, Free Press 2007, 173.
58 Roberts and Klibanoff, 179.
59 Counts, pg. xv.
60 Brodie copy of telegram received from Woody Mann.
61 As told to Brodie by Frank White and confirmed by his widow, Gay White, in a telephone conversation on June 23, 2007.
62 Halberstam, 667-690.
63 FBI Interview report, Eugene Newsom, Little Rock, Arkansas, September 11, 1957.
64 Halberstam, 667-690.
65 Bob Douglas, Editorial, *Arkansas Democrat-Gazette*, November 21, 1993.
66 Lee Riley Powell, *J. William Fulbright and His Times*, (Memphis, TN : Guild Bindery Press, 1996), 128.
67 Deborah Mathis, *Arkansas Democrat-Gazette*, December 17, 1994.
68 Halberstam, 667-690.
69 *Aaron vs. Cooper, Transcript of Proceedings, Friday September 20, 1957.*
    Aaron vs. Cooper as reported in 156 Federal Supplement at page 222.
    6. An injunction is necessary in order to preserve the judicial process of this Court, to maintain the due and proper administration of justice and to protect the rights guaranteed by the Constitution to the Negro children involved; now, therefore,
    It is hereby ordered and decreed that Defendant Orval E. Faubus, Governor of the State of Arkansas, General Sherman t. Clinger, Adjutant General of the State of Arkansas, and Lt. Col. Marion E. Johnson of the Arkansas National Guard, their officers, agents, servants, employees, attorneys, all persons subject to their joint or several orders and directions, and all persons in active concert, participation or privity with them, be and they are herby enjoined and restrained from hereafter (a) obstructing or preventing, by means of the Arkansas National Guard, or otherwise, Negro students, eligible under said plan of school integration to attend the Little rock Central High School, from attending said school or (b) from threatening or coercing said students not to attend said school or (c) from obstructing or interfering in any way with the carrying out and effectuation of this Court's orders of August 28, 1956, and September 3, 1957, in this cause, or (d) from otherwise obstructing and interfering with the constitutional right of said Negro children to attend said school.
    Provided that this Order shall not be deemed to prevent Orval E. Faubus, as Governor of the State of Arkansas, from taking any and all action he may deem necessary or desirable for the preservation of peace and order, by means of the Arkansas nation National Guard, or otherwise, which does not hinder or interfere with the right of eligible Negro students to attend the Little Rock Central High School.
70 *Arkansas Democrat-Gazette*, October 27, 1993.
71 Steele Hays and Ginger Shiras, "How Faubus Used State Police", *Arkansas Gazette*, June 3, 1979.

Chapter 3. The Consequences The Experienced

72 Elizabeth Eckford interview with CNN commemorating the 50th Anniversary of the 1954 *Brown* decision, 2004.
73 Halberstam, page 688.
74 Huckaby, xii.

75   Situation Analysis Report, Office of deputy Chief of Staff for Military Operations, March 1958

76   Statistics from *The Lost Year*, documentary by Sondra Gordy and Sandra Hubbard, based on data from the University of Arkansas Library Special Collections.

77   Ashmore, 133.

78   Ralph Brodie copy of speech given by a former faculty member at the 45th reunion of the Class of 1960.

79   Faculty member interview with Ralph Brodie August 27, 2006.

80   Ashmore, 133.

81   *Arkansas Gazette*, Editorial, February 12, 1958.

82   Henry M. Alexander, *The Little Rock Recall Election* (New York, McGraw Hill, 1960), 13.

83   *Arkansas Gazette*, Editorial, May 11, 1959.

84   Ibid.

85   Former Central High students at the University of Arkansas responsible for the statement of support for the purged teachers included: Howard "Buster" Jones and Ralph Brodie, Central's 1956-57 and 1957-58 student body presidents, respectively; Porter Briggs, Hall High's 1957-58 student body president who had attended Central as a sophomore and junior; Helen Ruth Smith Towns, captain of the Central's 1957-58 cheerleaders; and Barbara Barnes Broce, Central's 1957 Homecoming Queen.

86   Brodie copy of unpublished paper, The Stop Campaign by Frances Mitchell Ross, 1957 graduate of Central High and daughter of STOP chairman William Starr Mitchell.

87   Jacoway, 350.

88   Roberts and Klibanoff, 153.

89   Roberts and Klibanoff, 172.

90   *Arkansas Times*, September 12, 1997.

91   Halberstam, 684.

92   Gary Smith, "Blindsided by History", *Sports Illustrated*, April 9, 2007.

93   Huckaby, 27.

94   Smith.

95   Ibid.

Chapter 4. Personal Motivation

96   *Arkansas Democrat-Gazette*, October 5, 1997.

97   1st place, Little Rock Central High School Good Citizenship Award, Daughters of the American Revolution, Spring 1958.

98   Named "America's Most Beautiful High School" by the American Institute of Architects when built in 1927.

99   Little Rock Central High School, http://en.wikipedia.org/wiki/Little_Rock_Central_High_School.

100   Counts, 2.

101   Larry Taylor, in *Learning Together At Last, Memories Of The Desegregation Of The Arkansas Public School System*, ed. Paul Root, Pete Parks Center for Regional Studies, (Arkadelphia: Ouachita Baptist University, 2005).

102   Michael Carlson, "Woodrow Mann Obituary", *The National Guardian*, August 31, 2002.

103   Gene King, "Faces in the Graduating Class", *Arkansas Democrat*, May 25, 1958.

104   Editorial, *Arkansas Gazette*, October 6, 1957.

105   *The Tiger*, Vol. 62, No. 13, Thursday March 29, 1956, page 2.

106   Barry Sollenberger, *1988 Phoenix Metro Football*, 4-6, 62-70.

107   Barry Sollenberger, *2000 Phoenix Metro Football*, 86-87.

108 *Arkansas Democrat-Gazette*, Editorial "COACH, the legendary Wilson Matthews, 1921-2002", May 16, 2002

109 Ibid.

110 Confirmed in telephone conversation with Brodie on June 22, 2007.

111 Comments obtained through phone interview with Brodie, November14, 2002, and High Profile, *Arkansas Democrat-Gazette*, July 19, 1998.

Chapter 5. The Burden of Ethics

112 Ibid.

113 Brodie copy of letter by Little Rock attorneys.

114 Editorial, *Arkansas Gazette*, November 6, 1958.

115 *Arkansas Democrat-Gazette*, October 5, 1997, commentary originally printed in *The Washington Times*, September 26, 1997.

116 Leas.

117 James Scudder, *Arkansas Democrat*, October 3, 1979 and Meredith Oakley, Politics 1980.

About the Authors

Ralph Brodie graduated from Central High in 1958 ranked 33rd out of a class of 603 graduates. He was the Student Body President during the 1957-1958 school year. He attended the University of Arkansas in Fayetteville, on a track scholarship, and was the Student Body President in 1962-63. He graduated with a Bachelors of Science in Industrial Engineering in 1963 and a Juris Doctorate law degree in 1966. He later attended New York University where he earned a Master of Laws (in Taxation) in 1973. Brodie was inducted into the Arkansas Track & Field Hall of Fame in 2002, and into the Arkansas Academy of Industrial Engineers in 2005. He continues to live in Little Rock where he works as an Estate Planning and Tax lawyer. Since January 2006, he has served on Little Rock's 50th Anniversary Commission for the Desegregation of Little Rock Central High.

Marvin Schwartz is a New York native who has lived in Arkansas since 1971. He has a Master of Fine Arts in Poetry from the University of Arkansas. He has worked as a journalist, speechwriter, grants writer, director of nonprofit organizations, and instructor of English and creative writing in the U.S. and overseas. His writings have addressed a range of Arkansas public sector issues: rural development, community history and culture, civil rights, and education.

Printed in the United States
89998LV00003B/136-504/A